CALLIGRAPHY
STROKE BY STROKE

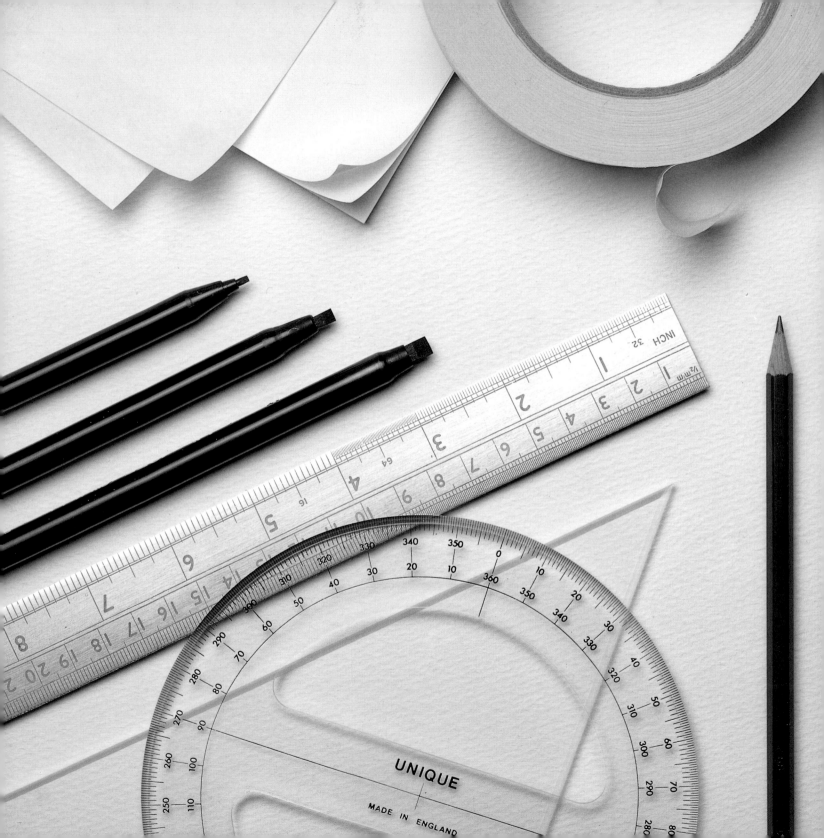

CALLIGRAPHY
STROKE BY
STROKE

A NEW ILLUSTRATED GUIDE
TO CALLIGRAPHY TECHNIQUES WITH
ELEVEN CALLIGRAPHIC ALPHABETS

Annie Moring

RUNNING PRESS
PHILADELPHIA • LONDON

A Quarto Book

Copyright © 1995 Quarto Inc.

All rights reserved under the Pan American and International Copyright Conventions. First published in the United States of America in 1995 by Running Press Book Publishers.

9 8 7 6 5 4 3 2 1

Digit on the right indicates the number of this printing.

ISBN 1-56138-537-9

Library of Congress Cataloging-in-Publication Number 95-67762

Designed and produced by
Quarto Inc.
The Old Brewery
6 Blundell Street
London N7 9BH

Senior editor *Maria Morgan*
Senior art editor *Penny Cobb*
Designers *Penny Dawes, Karin Skånberg*
Illustrations *Jane Hughes*
Diagrams *Dave Kemp*
Editor *Patricia Seligman*
Photographer *Paul Forrester*
Art director *Moira Clinch*
Editorial director *Mark Dartford*

Typeset by Central Southern Typesetters, East Sussex
Manufactured in Singapore by
Eray Scan Pte Ltd
Printed in Singapore by
Star Standard Industries (Pte) Ltd

This book may be ordered by mail from the publisher. Please include $2.50 for postage and handling. *But try your bookstore first!*

Running Press Book Publishers
125 South Twenty-second Street,
Philadelphia, Pennsylvania 19103-4399

CONTENTS

HOW TO USE THIS BOOK

After mastering the Beginners' Guide on pages 8–13, you will find that each alphabet section contains everything you need to start out in this practical art, from background information to finished inspirational examples.

Step-by-step photographs and diagrams show the formation of each letter.

Informational panels contain all the basic elements of each alphabet, such as letter height, slope, pen angle, "o" form, and type of serif.

THE ALPHABETS

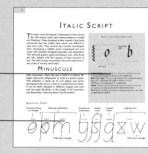

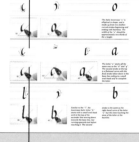

Geometric letter groupings are illustrated for the first five alphabets. The equivalent groupings for the remaining alphabets are listed in the information panels.

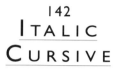

The pen angle is shown for each stroke of the individual letter.

TROUBLESHOOTING PAGES

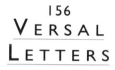

The complete alphabet shown in its correct form, but with a selection of badly written letters highlighted so that you can compare your own efforts and correct any mistakes.

Examples of incorrect letters and advice on avoiding common mistakes.

GALLERY PAGES

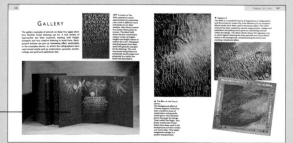

To stimulate your imagination, a gallery of finished work by contemporary calligraphers follows each alphabet.

INTRODUCTION

Calligraphy has become increasingly popular in recent years, and this book introduces the beginner to some of the most exciting calligraphic alphabets in both uppercase (majuscule) and lowercase (minuscule) forms. As your understanding of this art grows, so will your enjoyment.

Since the beginning of civilization, writing styles have always evolved with the tools and materials of the age – from prehistoric cave paintings when stones and sticks were used, to clay tablets, reed pens on papyrus, quill pens on parchment, to the metal pens on paper used today. Western scripts have developed over 2,000 years from the Roman alphabet which, in turn, evolved from the Greek. Carved inscriptions progressed to pen-made letters with the advent of manuscript books. The edged pen would give a thick-and-thin stroke, and the Uncial and Half Uncial styles were developed at a time of beautiful illumination. Rounder styles were followed by the Gothic alphabets, including Blackletter and Cursive, which were more compressed. The classical Roman letterforms were revived in the 15th and 16th centuries by Italian Renaissance scholars to produce a quicker, more flowing style known as Italic. An historical study of lettering gives the student a sound background, and special credit is due to Edward Johnston (1872–1944) for reviving the art of calligraphy in Britain through his researches into traditional book hands, his re-introduction of the square-cut pen, and his teaching first at the Central School of Art and then at the Royal College of Art. Many of his pupils went on to teach, and a very high proportion of today's professional calligraphers owe a lot to him. This revival soon spread to the United States and to other parts of Europe, and calligraphy is now truly international, with exciting lettering being created all over the world.

Although there will always be the traditionl work for the scribe such as presentation scrolls, memorial books, family trees, invitations, and certificates, lettering is now being used increasingly in advertising and graphic design. Creative new ideas using decorative and innovative surfaces, including fabrics, ceramics, and glass, and three-dimensional designs now offer endless possibilities whether for profit or for pleasure. I have enjoyed this art since childhood, and I hope that this book gives you the same pleasure.

Annie Moring

BEGINNERS' GUIDE

The best way to start is with all the necessary equipment close at hand and with a well-laid-out writing area. Good organization means fewer interruptions and more practice time. Make sure you understand the materials and feel comfortable with the equipment. The next stage is to acquire a clear understanding of historical letter shapes by studying the alphabets and galleries of finished artwork.

TOOLS AND MATERIALS

The increasing popularity of calligraphy has led to the availability of better and cheaper materials, including broad-edged felt-tip pens in a choice of colors, dip nibs, and a variety of calligraphic fountain pens. Most black and colored inks, if non-waterproof, can be used with a fountain pen, and watercolors, gouache, and even water-based acrylics can be used with dip pens.

Calligraphic paper ranges from practice layout and cartridge paper to machine-made, pastel, mold-made, handmade, and parchment papers. Your choice will depend on the project in mind, but always check what's available in your local art store.

CHECKLIST

1 **Paper** Experiment with different surfaces and weights, but avoid highly coated or glossy paper.

2 **Masking tape** Used for taping together pencils and for securing the writing paper.

3 **Felt-tip pens** The larger sizes are particularly ideal for practicing after double pencils.

4 **Rulers** Keep a long metal ruler for drawing lines. A T-square is also useful.

5 **L-square** Squaring up is easier with a transparent plastic L-square.

6 **Protractor** Use a clear plastic protractor to check angles.

7 **Double pencils** To get the idea of a calligraphic pen, tape together two pencils to make "double letters." Make sure that the points are level, unless you are left-handed. If the pencils move about, carefully shave down one side of each before joining them. They will then be easier to manage and give smaller letterforms.

8 **Pencils** Ordinary lead pencils give sharp but easily erasable lines.

WRITING POSITION

To begin with, you should sit at a solid table or desk in a position which is comfortable, with a chair of the correct height, with supports for the back and which allows you to place your feet flat on the floor. A board is best positioned at an angle of approximately 45° as this gives a clear view of the whole working area and allows the ink to flow more easily. The board need not be an expensive piece of equipment; a drawing board positioned on your lap and leaning against a table works well. In time you might consider investing in a designer's drawing board which can be altered to different angles.

Good natural daylight is best to see by, but the next best thing is to work in a room with daylight bulbs. If you are working under artificial light, it should come from the left if you are right-handed, and vice versa, to ensure that there are no shadows on the writing area.

PREPARING THE BOARD

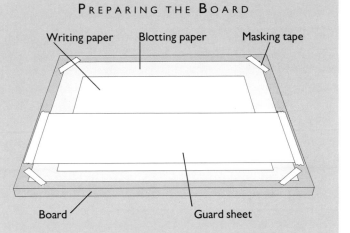

Writing paper Blotting paper Masking tape

Board Guard sheet

The drawing board can now be prepared for writing. First tape several sheets of soft paper, preferably blotting paper, to the board so that it has some give. A guard sheet is then put on just below the writing level to prevent any dirt or grease from your hands getting onto the writing paper. The writing paper is then slipped under the guard, which will hold it firm while allowing it to be adjusted to maintain a constant writing level.

SEATING POSITION

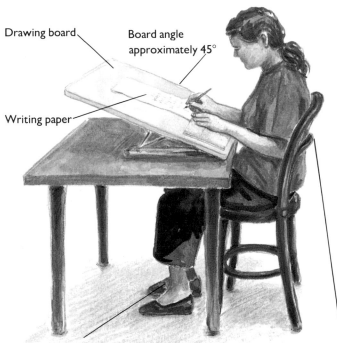

Drawing board

Board angle approximately 45°

Writing paper

Comfortable chair allowing both your feet to be flat on the floor

Supports the back

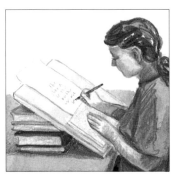

Prop board against books

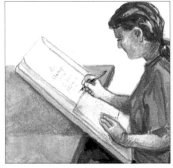

Rest the board in your lap

▶ *Practice holding double pencils and making flowing parallel strokes. Left-handers should keep one point slightly higher.*

RULING

The writing paper needs guidelines, and "H" graded pencils are particularly useful: 2H or 3H kept very sharp will give a clear yet thin line allowing the measuring to be more accurate. A ruler and L-square will help keep the lines straight.

The writing height, or x height, which is the size of the lowercase letters without ascenders or descenders, depends on the alphabet and nib size used. For example, the Foundational lowercase letters are 4½ times the width of the nib. To work this out, rule a line, then holding the pen upright, make horizontal blocks like steps, one on top of another to make a "ladder," until 4½ is reached. This is then measured to give you the writing height for the nib size that you are using. Larger nibs are better to start with as they are easier to control and the letters can be seen clearly and mistakes corrected.

Having established the x height, add the ascender and descender lines for those parts of the letters that extend above and below the x height, like the vertical lines of "b" and "p." For the Foundational lowercase these lines are 2½ nib widths above and below the x height.

ESSENTIAL INFORMATION

Make sure you are familiar with all the basic elements of letterforms and with how they differ throughout the individual alphabets. Pay particular attention to letter heights, pen angles, letter slopes, and serif forms to ensure consistency in your writing. Use these basic elements in conjunction with the step-by-step diagrams, checking carefully for any changes to these elements and for unusual stroke directions.

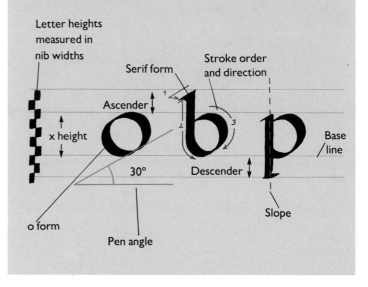

RULING UP WITH DOUBLE PENCILS

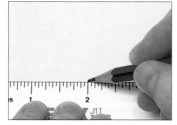

1 *Beginners should first master ruling up using double pencils, following the technique shown, before progressing to felt-tip pens. Begin by ruling a single line approximately 2 inches from the top of your page. This will give you plenty of room for the double pencils.*

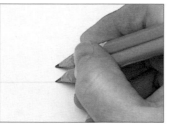

2 *Hold the two pencils together with the points level. If you are left-handed, keep the first pencil slightly lower to give a left oblique angle. Tape the pencils together at the top and bottom and hold them upright on the pencil base line.*

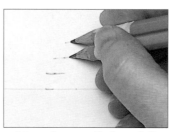

3 *Move the pencils from left to right to form horizontal lines. Now proceed to the top of the first stroke and, touching it, add another line. Repeat this 4½ times to form a staircase, giving you the x height for the Foundational hand.*

WITH A FELT-TIP PEN

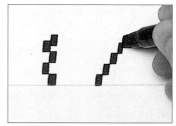

Begin as before by ruling a single line 2 inches from the top of the page. To set up the letter height using nib widths, hold the nib vertically and form a ladder or staircase of the required number of nib widths, in this case 4½.

STROKE ORDER

To construct a letter correctly, follow the instructions given, using the diagrams and photographs. The strokes are numbered, and the direction of the stroke is also indicated, as it is not always as expected.

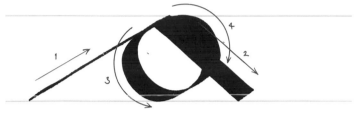

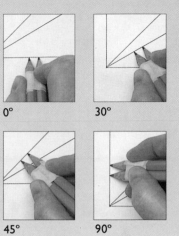

PEN ANGLES

The angle of your nib depends on the alphabet being copied. For example, Foundational hand is written with the nib at 30° to the horizontal writing line. This nib angle dictates the thick and thin strokes, and keeping it constant requires practice. Start with curves, verticals, horizontals, and combined strokes, keeping them as even as possible.

0°   30°   45°   90°

DOUBLE PENCIL STROKES

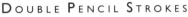

1 *Begin by ruling your lines for double pencils as shown left. Now move from left to right at a 30° angle from the base line up to the top line, making sure that both pencils are touching the paper. This should give you a single thin line as the two pencils follow one another. If a double line appears, check the angle with a protractor.*
2 *Keeping the angle constant, proceed diagonally to the right and down to the base line; this will give a double line. A felt-tip pen will produce a single thin line followed by a thick line the total width of the nib.*
3 *Practice a series of left- and right-hand curves, joining them later to form the letter "O." Added to your thin and thick pyramid exercises, this helps to keep the angle correct. Vertical and horizontal lines at this 30° angle can now be included.*

FELT-TIP STROKES

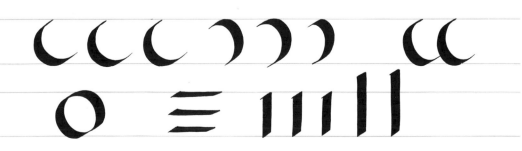

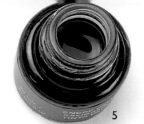

1 **Fountain pens** Available with interchangeable nibs; use them with cartridge ink or with a refillable chamber.

2 **Pen holders** Make sure that the nib fits securely.

3 **Nibs** Round-hand, square-cut nibs range from size 0 to 6, 0 being the largest. Left-oblique nibs give the clearest finishes.

4 **Reservoirs** Clip-on types fit underneath the round-hand nibs about ⅛ inch from the tip.

5 **Ink and paints** Start with non-waterproof black ink like India or Chinese ink, experimenting later with colored inks, watercolors, or liquid acrylic paints. Gouache paints give a soft, opaque finish.

BEGINNING TO WRITE

A comfortable position to hold your pen is quite close to the nib, resting it on the first joint of the middle finger and holding it in place with the thumb and index finger. Relax your hand and try not to grip the pen too tightly. This will allow greater flexibility and movement.

Fill the pen either by dipping it into the ink as far as the two holes at the back of the reservoir or by using a brush to feed in the ink from one side, in between the nib and the reservoir. To make sure that you have the correct pen angle to the writing line, a protractor can be used to rule very faint lines on your practice sheet at the appropriate angle for the alphabet.

LEFT HANDERS

Round-hand dip nibs are available in all left-oblique sizes, and most brands of fountain pens are also easily available. Steeper pen angles may be required to achieve the necessary thick and thin strokes.

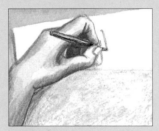

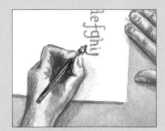

Hook position Slanting the paper down to the left may help.

Vertical position Try placing the paper at 90° to the horizontal, working from top to bottom.

PEN STROKES

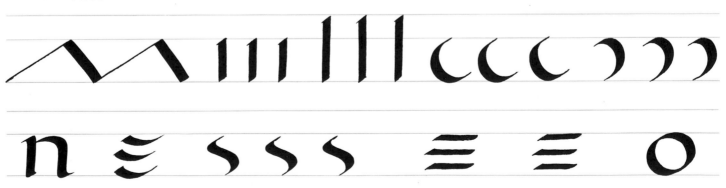

"O" FORM

The shape of the letter "o" is often the key to the rest of the alphabet. It is from the "o" that the arch, the slant (slope), and the shape of the serifs derive. Thus you will see the rounded arch of the "o" in the letters "m" and "n" and side curves in letters "a" and "b," and so on.

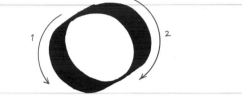

GEOMETRIC FORMS

Alphabets which can be related to Roman capitals can be understood geometrically and grouped into letter shapes. The letter "o" is theoretically a perfect circle within a square, and similar letters can be grouped together, making alphabets easier to understand. Other letters take up three-quarters of the width of a square and some half the width; one or two letters are very narrow or very wide. Geometric forms are illustrated for the first five alphabets in the book. The letter groupings for the remaining scripts, which do not conform easily geometrically, are described in the information panels.

Letter grouping is most important to all alphabets, as it will help you to understand how the letters are formed as well as allowing the letters to be uniform. Letters which contain diagonals, for instance, would be constructed and grouped together, as would letters which start with a straight side and then arch.

SLOPE

The slope of a letter is measured as the slant of a down-stroke to a vertical line. For example, Foundational hand is written upright, but an Italic style is written at a 5° angle. To maintain this slant throughout your writing in Italic, rule 5° lines on the writing paper as guidelines.

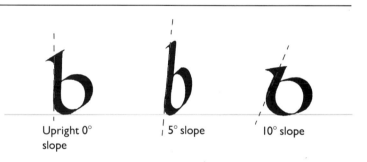

Upright 0° slope

5° slope

10° slope

SERIFS

Serifs are the starting and finishing strokes of letters and are usually related to the shape of the letters written. For example, the Foundational lowercase serifs are round, the Italic oval, and so on, relating to the "o" form. Although there can be more than one type of serif used, such as triangular, flag, or slab, they must be in character with the alphabet being written. The following are examples of the different serif forms used in this book.

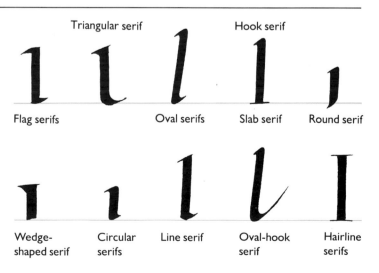

Triangular serif

Hook serif

Flag serifs

Oval serifs

Slab serif

Round serif

Wedge-shaped serif

Circular serifs

Line serif

Oval-hook serif

Hairline serifs

THE ALPHABETS

The first alphabet in this book is the Foundational hand because it is probably the best lower-case learning hand in use today. Together with the capitals, it teaches pen control, balance and legibility.

The Italic script allows more speed and flourish, and is considered the most useful and versatile script in use today. The beauty and elegance of the Roman Capitals are followed by the gracefully rounded Uncial and Half Uncial styles. The rhythm of the Gothic style teaches better spacing techniques and is followed by Italic cursive. Versal capital letters, which can be used as initial letters with most styles, complete the alphabets.

FOUNDATIONAL LOWER CASE

abcdefghijklm

nopqrstuvwxyz

FOUNDATIONAL CAPITALS

ABCDEFGHIJKLM

NOPQRSTUVWXYZ

ITALIC MINUSCULE

abcdefghijklm
nopqrstuvwxyz

ITALIC CAPITALS

ABCDEFGHIJKLM
NOPQRSTUVWXYZ

ROMAN CAPITALS

ABCDEFGHIJKLM
NOPQRSTUVWXYZ

MODERN UNCIAL

aBCDEFGhIJKLM

NOPQRSTUVWXYZ

HALF UNCIAL

abcdefghijklm

NOPQRSTUVWXYZ

GOTHIC LOWER CASE

abcdefghijklm

nopqrstuvwxyz

GOTHIC CAPITALS

ABCDEFGHIJKLM

NOPQRSTUVWXYZ

ITALIC CURSIVE

abcdefghijklm

nopqrstuvwxyz

VERSAL LETTERS

ABCDEFGHIJKLM

NOPQRSTUVWXYZ

FOUNDATIONAL HAND

The late 19th century saw the growth of the Arts and Crafts Movement in England. Its aim was to revive craftsmanship lost through industrialization. Two such crafts were calligraphy and illumination – the decoration with color and gold leaf of the calligraphy.

Edward Johnston (1872–1944), moving from Edinburgh and encouraged by the Movement, developed a new style of writing, the Foundational hand, based on ancient manuscripts seen in the British Museum. His book *Writing and Illuminating and Lettering,* published in 1906, is still considered to be the "Calligrapher's Bible."

LOWERCASE

The letterforms of the Foundational hand lower case are curved bowls based on a circle with straight vertical stems. Most of the stems are topped with triangular serifs and end with small circular serifs, allowing the letters to be joined if required. The roundness and constant 30° angle required to write this hand make it an obvious choice for the learning calligrapher.

ESSENTIAL INFORMATION

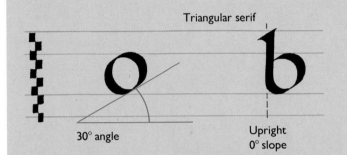

Triangular serif

30° angle

Upright
0° slope

Letter height The x height is 4½ nib widths, and the ascenders and descenders are an extra 2½ nib widths each.
Basic pen angle The pen angle between the nib and the writing line is 30°. However, for the diagonal strokes of the "v," "w," and "x," the angle should be steepened to 45°.
"O" form This alphabet has a circular "o."
Slope This is an upright alphabet; that is to say that the letters are constructed vertical to the writing line.
Serif forms Triangular serifs are used, with small circular serifs which echo the circular shape of the letter "o."

GEOMETRIC FORMS

Circular letters | Three-quarter width letters | Letters with diagonals | Straight-sided arched letters

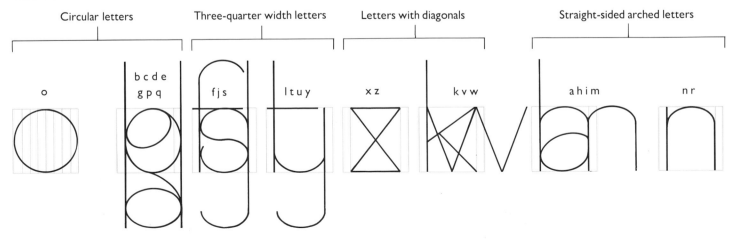

o

bcde
gpq

fjs

ltuy

xz

kvw

ahim

nr

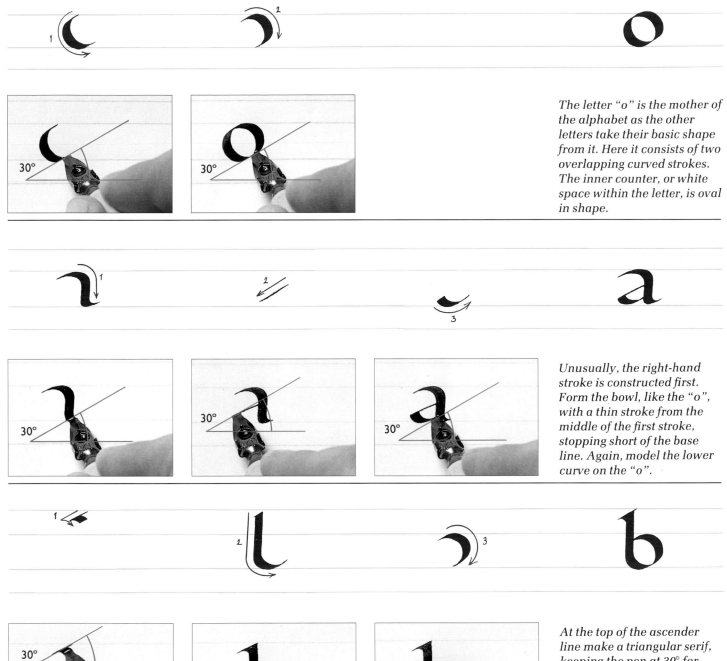

The letter "o" is the mother of the alphabet as the other letters take their basic shape from it. Here it consists of two overlapping curved strokes. The inner counter, or white space within the letter, is oval in shape.

Unusually, the right-hand stroke is constructed first. Form the bowl, like the "o", with a thin stroke from the middle of the first stroke, stopping short of the base line. Again, model the lower curve on the "o".

At the top of the ascender line make a triangular serif, keeping the pen at 30° for your vertical downstroke and curving to the right just before the base line. The final stroke is like the "o", joining the bottom curve.

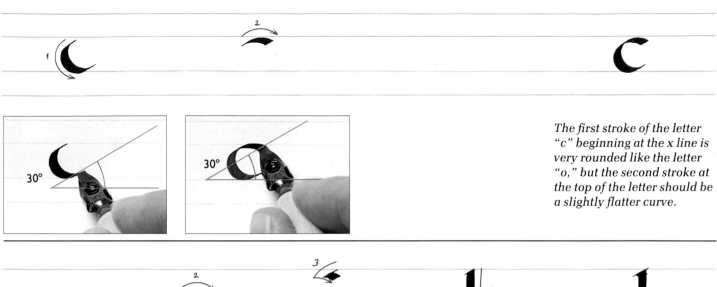

The first stroke of the letter "c" beginning at the x line is very rounded like the letter "o," but the second stroke at the top of the letter should be a slightly flatter curve.

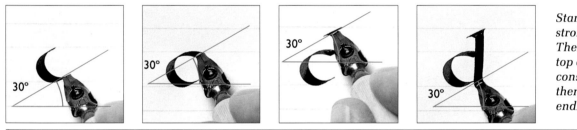

Start with the first two strokes of the letter "c." Then, taking the pen to the top of the ascender line, construct the triangular serif, then the vertical downstroke ending with a circular serif.

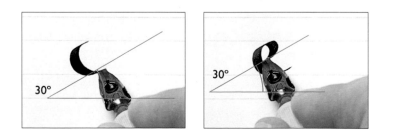

The letter "e" is based on the letter "o." The second stroke, however, curves inward, hitting the first stroke just above halfway.

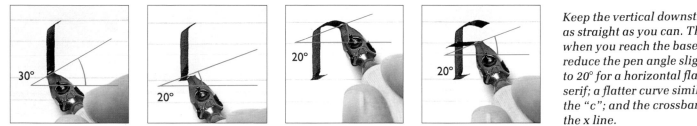

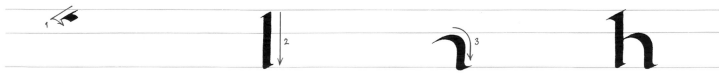

Keep the vertical downstroke as straight as you can. Then, when you reach the base line, reduce the pen angle slightly to 20° for a horizontal flag serif; a flatter curve similar to the "c"; and the crossbar on the x line.

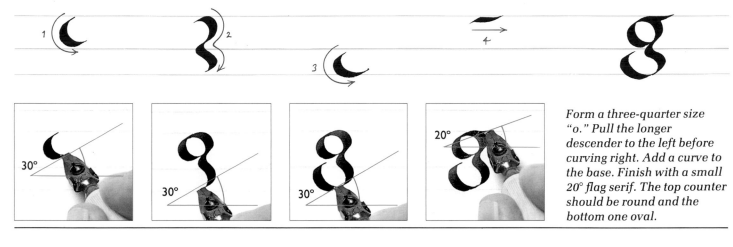

Form a three-quarter size "o." Pull the longer descender to the left before curving right. Add a curve to the base. Finish with a small 20° flag serif. The top counter should be round and the bottom one oval.

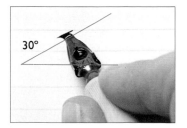
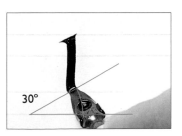
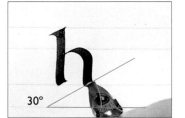

Start with the triangular serif ascender line, add a vertical downstroke and end on the base line with a small circular serif. The final stroke arches from within the stem and ends with a circular serif.

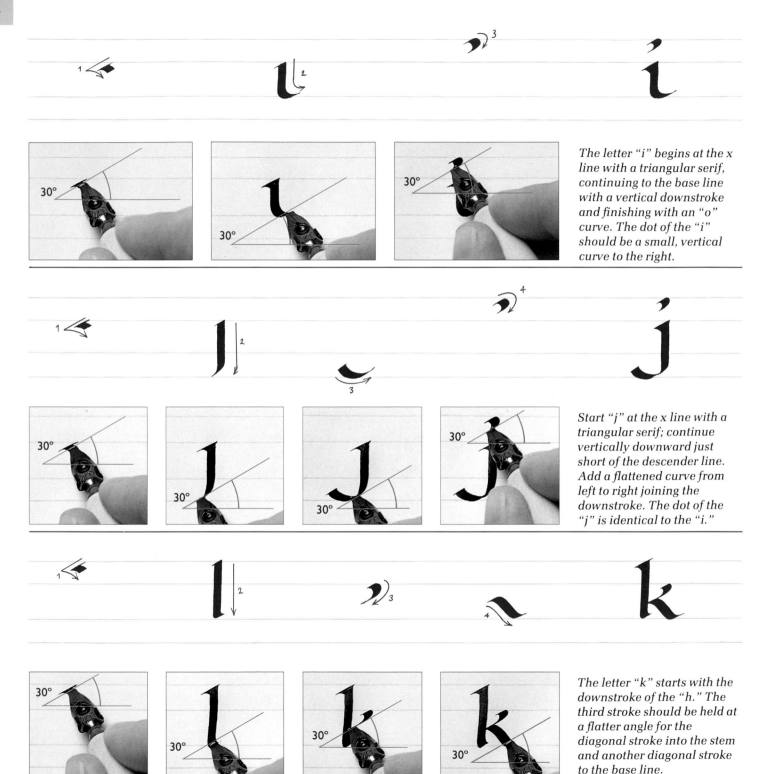

The letter "i" begins at the x line with a triangular serif, continuing to the base line with a vertical downstroke and finishing with an "o" curve. The dot of the "i" should be a small, vertical curve to the right.

Start "j" at the x line with a triangular serif; continue vertically downward just short of the descender line. Add a flattened curve from left to right joining the downstroke. The dot of the "j" is identical to the "i."

The letter "k" starts with the downstroke of the "h." The third stroke should be held at a flatter angle for the diagonal stroke into the stem and another diagonal stroke to the base line.

Keep the letter "l" as upright as possible; never allow your writing to slope backward. After the triangular serif, continue with the vertical downstroke, finishing with a generous curve at the bottom of the letter.

Take a vertical downstroke to the base line; end with a small circular serif. Add two identical arches springing from within the letter stem, again finishing with small circular serifs. The two halves should be equal.

The first stroke of the letter "n" is vertical, ending on the base line with a small circular serif. The second stroke, the arch of the letter, should spring from within the letter stem at the point where the serif and upright meet.

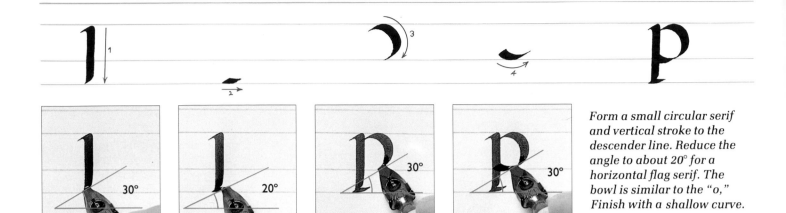

Form a small circular serif and vertical stroke to the descender line. Reduce the angle to about 20° for a horizontal flag serif. The bowl is similar to the "o," Finish with a shallow curve.

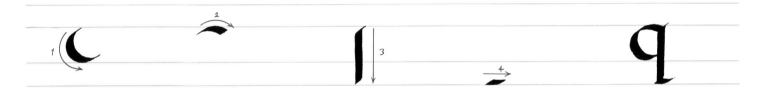

Start the letter "q" with the first two strokes of the letter "c" and continue with a vertical downstroke to the descender line. Slightly reduce the pen angle to 20° for a horizontal flag serif.

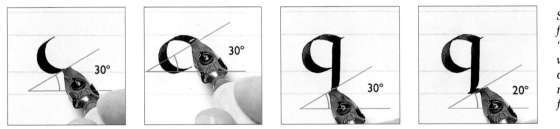

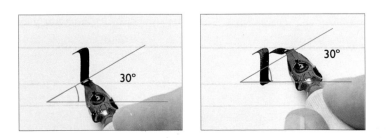

Start as for "n," continuing vertically to the base line and ending with another small circular serif. The second small stroke branches from the stem and arches minimally before ending with an upward flick.

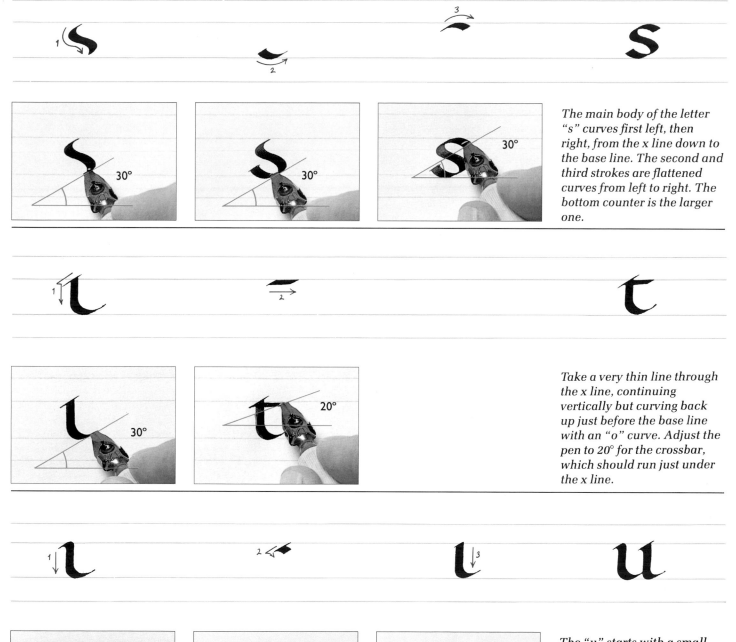

The main body of the letter "s" curves first left, then right, from the x line down to the base line. The second and third strokes are flattened curves from left to right. The bottom counter is the larger one.

Take a very thin line through the x line, continuing vertically but curving back up just before the base line with an "o" curve. Adjust the pen to 20° for the crossbar, which should run just under the x line.

The "u" starts with a small circular serif with a down-stroke curving up like "t." The second and third strokes have a triangular serif, then a vertical downstroke ending with a circular serif on the base line.

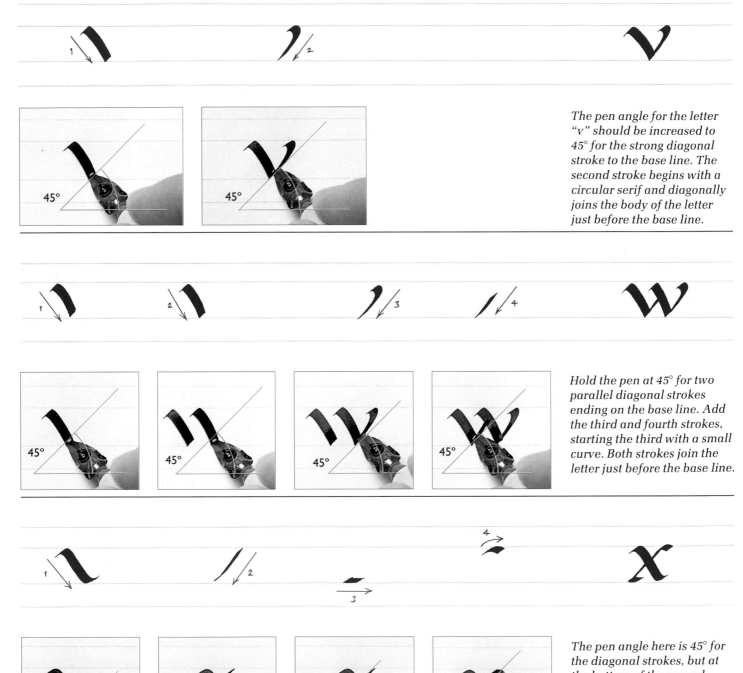

The pen angle for the letter "v" should be increased to 45° for the strong diagonal stroke to the base line. The second stroke begins with a circular serif and diagonally joins the body of the letter just before the base line.

Hold the pen at 45° for two parallel diagonal strokes ending on the base line. Add the third and fourth strokes, starting the third with a small curve. Both strokes join the letter just before the base line.

The pen angle here is 45° for the diagonal strokes, but at the bottom of the second stroke, the angle changes to approximately 20° for a horizontal flag serif. The fourth stroke is a small circular serif.

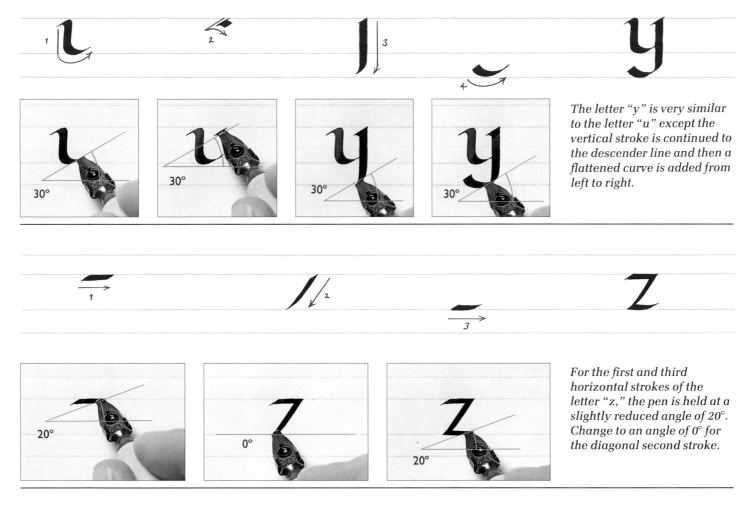

The letter "y" is very similar to the letter "u" except the vertical stroke is continued to the descender line and then a flattened curve is added from left to right.

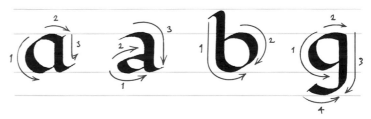

For the first and third horizontal strokes of the letter "z," the pen is held at a slightly reduced angle of 20°. Change to an angle of 0° for the diagonal second stroke.

ALTERNATIVES

Some letters in the Foundational lower-case alphabet have alternative letter and serif forms. Make sure, however, that, if these alternative forms are used, they are consistent throughout the piece of work.

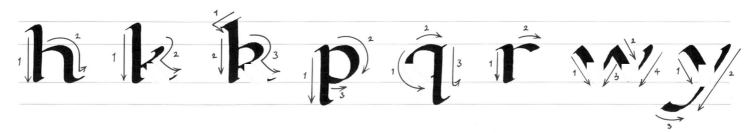

TROUBLESHOOTING

As this is usually the first alphabet that the beginner copies, special attention needs to be given to the consistency of family characteristics. This means checking that curves are the same and not overdoing the serifs, making them too large. Try to keep the vertical downstrokes upright as there is a tendency to construct these leaning backward. The inner spaces of letters need to be balanced as well, such as those of the "n" and "u." With the letter "m," both inner areas should be equal.

The top diagonal stroke of the letter "k" is too small and the second diagonal is too long.

CORRECT LETTERFORMS

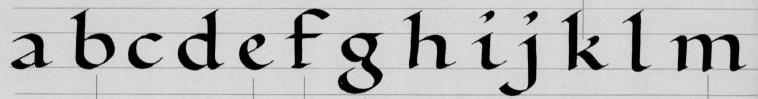

The serif at the top of the ascender of the letter "b" is far too large.

The top curve of the letter "e" joins the body of the letter too high up, leaving the counter space too small.

The top "o" shape of the letter "g" should be three quarters of the x height from the top. Here it is too big, giving the letter a top-heavy appearance.

The second arch of the letter "m" has been constructed too near the first so that the two sides, therefore, are not equal.

The horizontal crossbar of the letter "f" has been constructed too high up the letter. It should be on the x line.

The diagonal strokes of this "x" cross too high up the letter.

The top curve of the letter "s" is too long, which makes the letter look as if it is falling over.

The top counter space of the letter "s" is far too small and does not balance the letter.

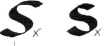

n o p q r s t u v w x y z

The bottom serif of the letter "p" has been constructed at too steep an angle, making it too heavy.

The diagonal stroke of the letter "z" has been written with the pen held at too steep an angle, making it too narrow.

The letter "n" has been constructed with the bottom curved serifs over-exaggerated, making the letter appear too narrow.

The vertical elements of this letter have been constructed too close together, which makes it look too narrow.

CAPITALS

Foundational hand capitals are based on the geometric principles of the Roman capital *quadrata,* using a circle, square and proportions of them. Very rounded shapes and small flag serifs give this majuscule hand a simple and neat appearance, which makes it easily legible and particularly suitable for headings.

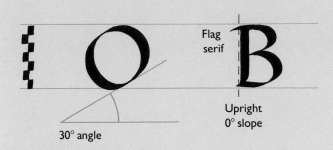

ESSENTIAL INFORMATION

Flag serif
Upright 0° slope
30° angle

Letter height This alphabet is 7 nib widths high.
Basic pen angle Usually 30°, but 20°, and 45° also used.
"O" form Circular.
Slope This is an upright alphabet.
Serif forms Flag serifs have been used with small circular serifs.

GEOMETRIC FORMS

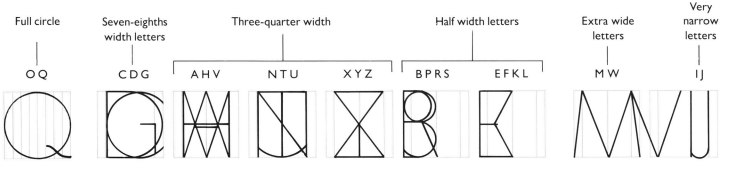

Full circle	Seven-eighths width letters	Three-quarter width			Half width letters		Extra wide letters	Very narrow letters
O Q	C D G	A H V	N T U	X Y Z	B P R S	E F K L	M W	I J

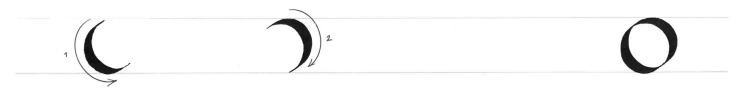

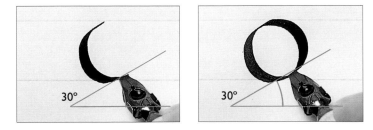

30°   30°

For this alphabet, and therefore the "O," the pen is held at a 30° angle. The left-hand curve is constructed first, beginning as a hairline and gradually thickening, curving and finishing again with a hairline. Start the

right-hand curve part way in the first, following the curve around the top and bringing it down to touch the hairline at the bottom. The outer shape of the "O" is based on a circle, but the inner counter should be an oval.

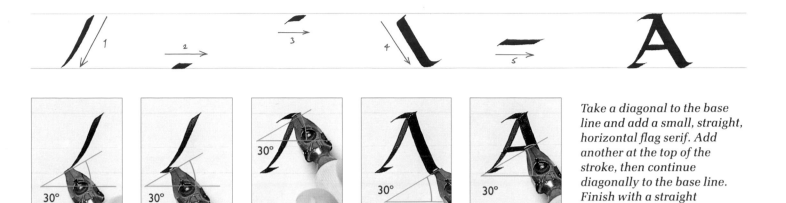

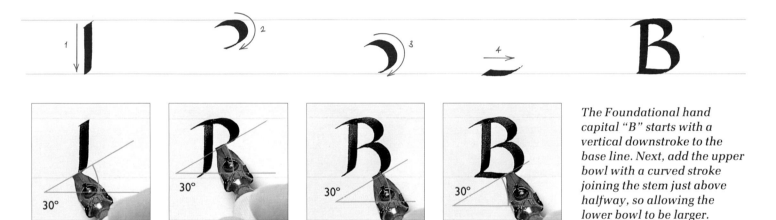

Take a diagonal to the base line and add a small, straight, horizontal flag serif. Add another at the top of the stroke, then continue diagonally to the base line. Finish with a straight crossbar below halfway.

The Foundational hand capital "B" starts with a vertical downstroke to the base line. Next, add the upper bowl with a curved stroke joining the stem just above halfway, so allowing the lower bowl to be larger.

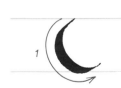

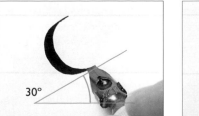

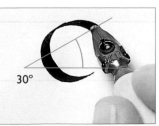

Like the "O," this begins with a hairline just below the x line, thickening and curving around to end with another hairline. The second stroke comes from within the first to form the top of the letter with a slightly flattened curve.

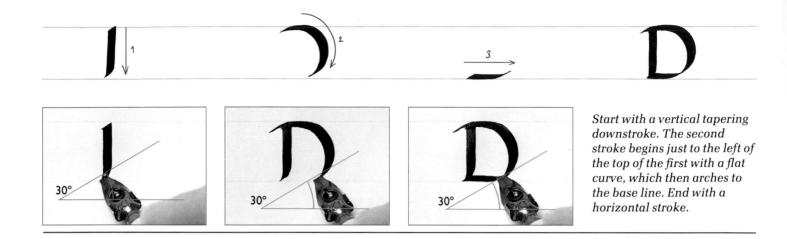

Start with a vertical tapering downstroke. The second stroke begins just to the left of the top of the first with a flat curve, which then arches to the base line. End with a horizontal stroke.

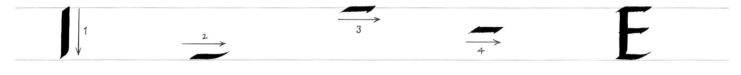

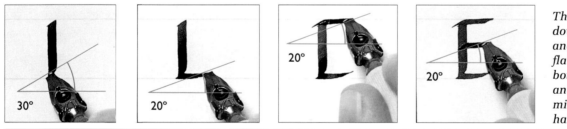

This consists of a vertical downstroke to the base line and three horizontal bars at a flatter 20° angle. Note that the bottom bar is slightly longer and more tapered and the middle bar slightly above halfway.

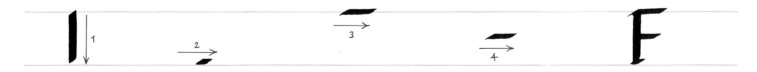

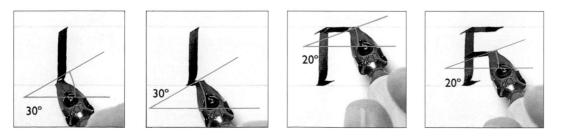

Like the letter "E," the letter "F" begins with a vertical downstroke to the base line, but then a small flag serif is added. Two horizontal bars complete the letter, the middle bar on, or slightly below, the center of the stem.

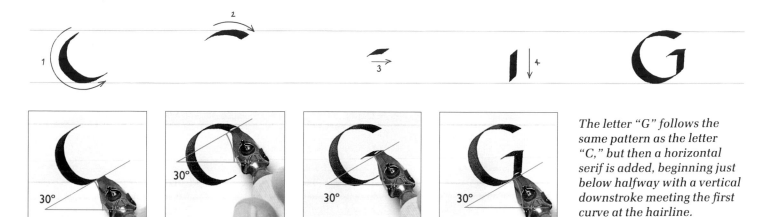

The letter "G" follows the same pattern as the letter "C," but then a horizontal serif is added, beginning just below halfway with a vertical downstroke meeting the first curve at the hairline.

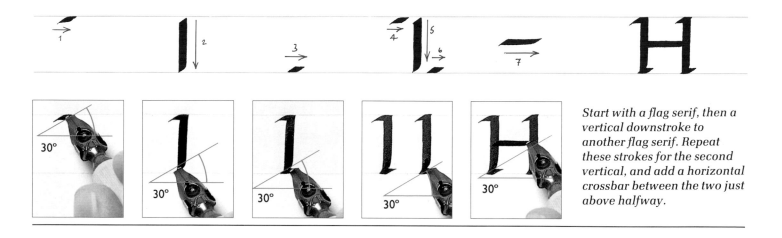

Start with a flag serif, then a vertical downstroke to another flag serif. Repeat these strokes for the second vertical, and add a horizontal crossbar between the two just above halfway.

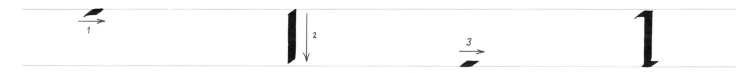

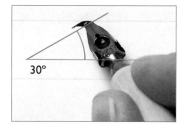

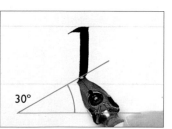

The letter "I" starts with a flag serif at the top of the cap line before dropping vertically down to the base line where a further flag serif is added.

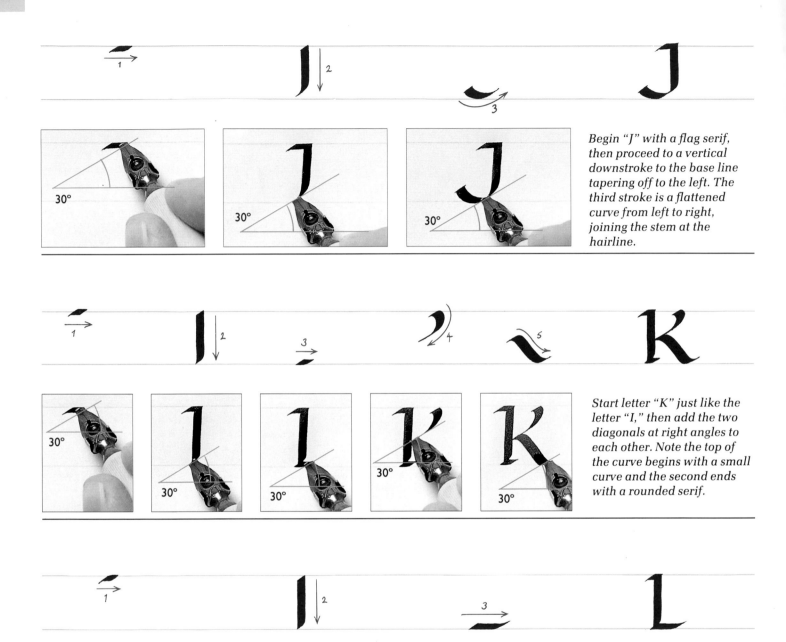

Begin "J" with a flag serif, then proceed to a vertical downstroke to the base line tapering off to the left. The third stroke is a flattened curve from left to right, joining the stem at the hairline.

Start letter "K" just like the letter "I," then add the two diagonals at right angles to each other. Note the top of the curve begins with a small curve and the second ends with a rounded serif.

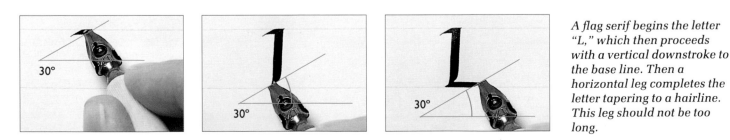

A flag serif begins the letter "L," which then proceeds with a vertical downstroke to the base line. Then a horizontal leg completes the letter tapering to a hairline. This leg should not be too long.

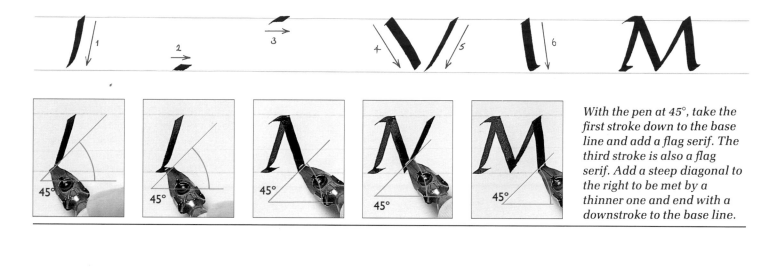

With the pen at 45°, take the first stroke down to the base line and add a flag serif. The third stroke is also a flag serif. Add a steep diagonal to the right to be met by a thinner one and end with a downstroke to the base line.

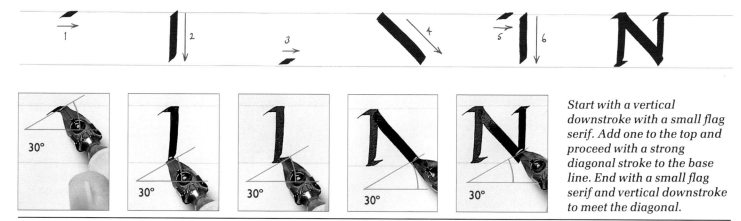

Start with a vertical downstroke with a small flag serif. Add one to the top and proceed with a strong diagonal stroke to the base line. End with a small flag serif and vertical downstroke to meet the diagonal.

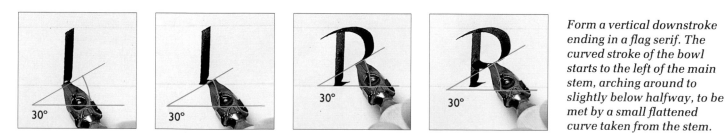

Form a vertical downstroke ending in a flag serif. The curved stroke of the bowl starts to the left of the main stem, arching around to slightly below halfway, to be met by a small flattened curve taken from the stem.

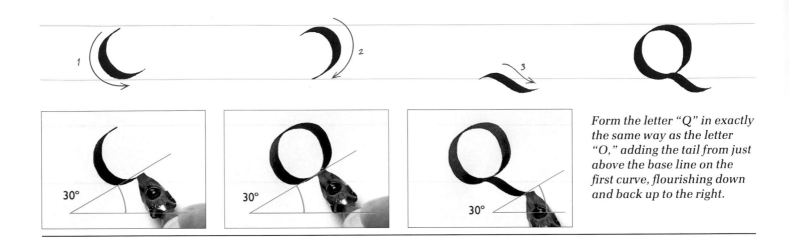

Form the letter "Q" in exactly the same way as the letter "O," adding the tail from just above the base line on the first curve, flourishing down and back up to the right.

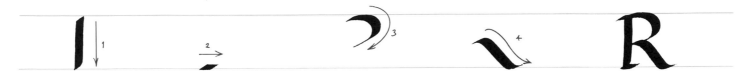

Start in the same way as the letter "P." Then take the bowl stroke round in a hairline toward the stem. Add the diagonal tail stroke springing out of the stem to the base line to finish with a gentle, tapering upturn.

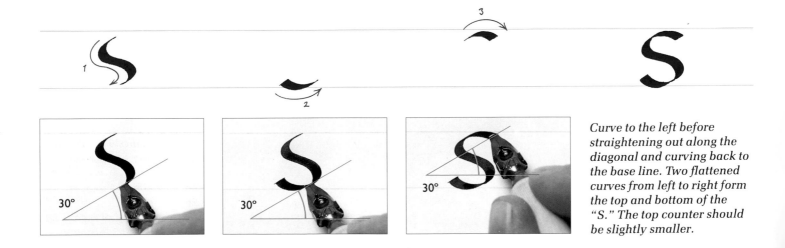

Curve to the left before straightening out along the diagonal and curving back to the base line. Two flattened curves from left to right form the top and bottom of the "S." The top counter should be slightly smaller.

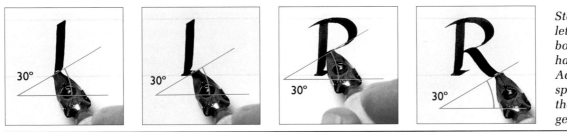

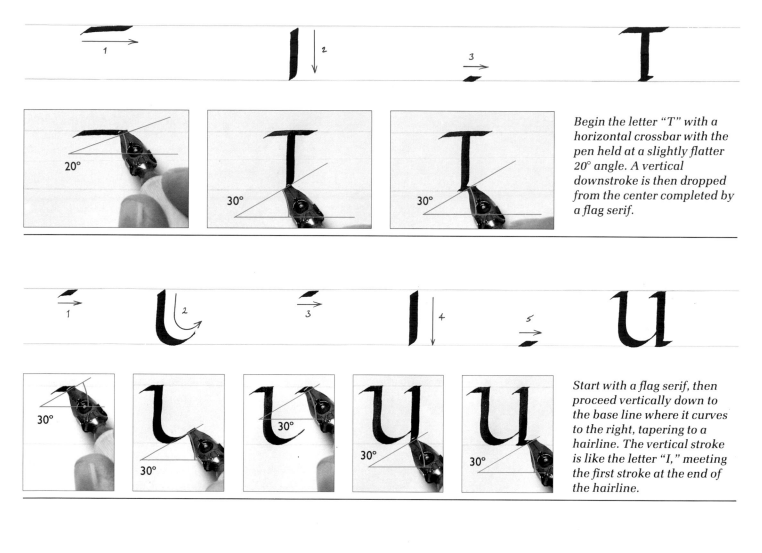

Begin the letter "T" with a horizontal crossbar with the pen held at a slightly flatter 20° angle. A vertical downstroke is then dropped from the center completed by a flag serif.

Start with a flag serif, then proceed vertically down to the base line where it curves to the right, tapering to a hairline. The vertical stroke is like the letter "I," meeting the first stroke at the end of the hairline.

The pen angle for the letter "V" should be steepened to 45° for the two diagonal strokes. Start the second stroke with a small round serif and continue diagonally down to join the bottom of the first stroke.

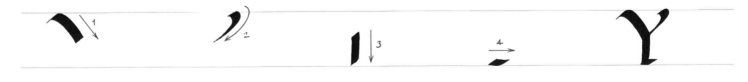

Like "V," construct the letter "W" using a 45° angle, with the first two diagonals parallel. The third stroke starts with a small round serif and joins the base of the second stroke. Finally, join the first two strokes together.

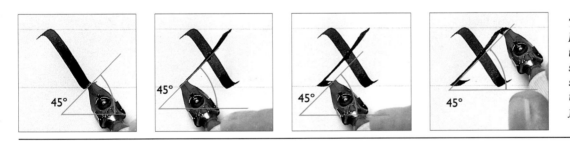

The diagonal strokes of the letter "X" are written with the pen at 45° crossing slightly above halfway. A flag serif is added to the bottom of the second stroke and a flattened curve to the top.

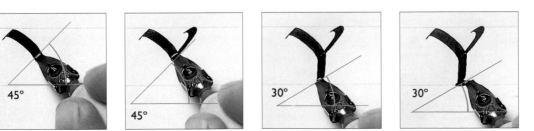

With the pen at 45°, take a diagonal from the cap line to the x line. Add the second diagonal, which starts with a small round serif. Finish with a vertical stroke to the base line and a flag serif.

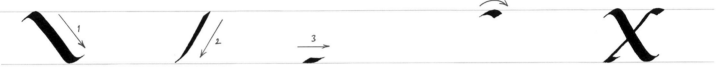

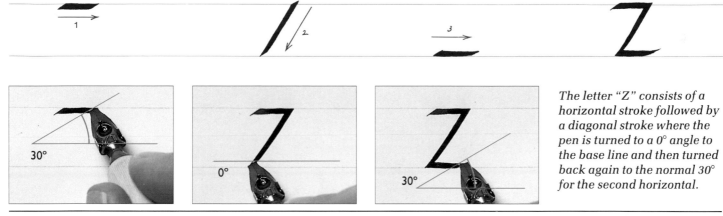

The letter "Z" consists of a horizontal stroke followed by a diagonal stroke where the pen is turned to a 0° angle to the base line and then turned back again to the normal 30° for the second horizontal.

ALTERNATIVES

Within this alphabet there are not only alternative letters, but also various serif forms – triangular, round, and flag. Numbers and punctuation marks are adapted to suit the alphabet written. Numbers, however, can be either ranged, that is the same height as the capitals, or non-ranged. A third option is the antique style which has ascenders and descenders to match the lower case.

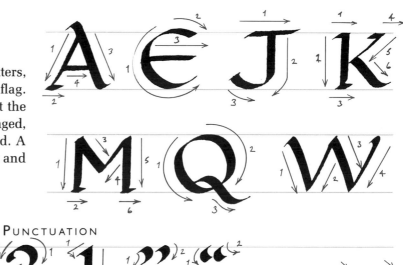

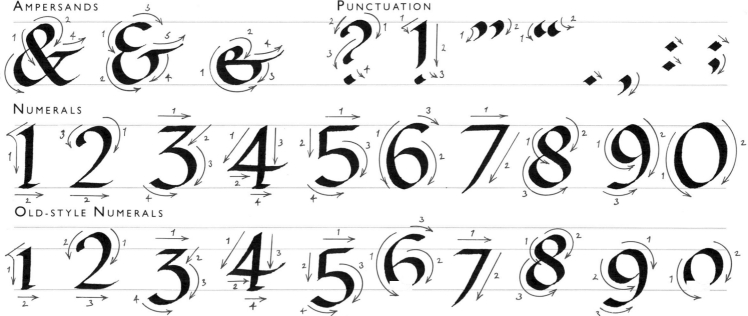

Troubleshooting

When constructing Foundational capitals, make sure that the serifs are not too large and that they are at the correct angle. Crossbars often cause problems, too, particularly with the capital "A" and "H" where they are usually positioned either too high up or too low down the letter. The capital "T" also looks top-heavy if the crossbar is constructed at the wrong angle. Another problem concerns balancing the letter "B." Make sure that your first curve enters the stem just above halfway, making the top bowl smaller than the bottom one.

The top serif and the bottom horizontal of the letter "L" are too wavy and should be straight.

Take care to set the verticals of the letter "H" far enough apart. Here they are too close and the crossbar too high, so it appears out of proportion.

Correct Letterforms

ABCDEFGHIJKLM

The horizontal crossbar of the letter "A" has been constructed too high up the letter, giving it an unbalanced look.

With the horizontal crossbar of the letter "A" too low down, it again looks unbalanced.

Here the diagonals are set too far apart, which gives the letter a collapsed appearance.

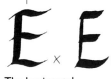

The horizontal arms of the letter "E" are wavy and should be very straight.

This letter "E" has been constructed with the pen at too steep an angle, making the horizontals too heavy and the vertical too narrow.

The top and bottom flag serifs of this letter are waved and should be straight.

Here the top flattened curve of the letter "S" is far too small and the bottom curve too long, making the letter unbalanced. These should be the same length.

S×

The horizontal strokes of the letter "Z" wave too much instead of being straight.

Z×

NOPQRSTUVWXYZ

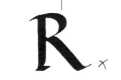

R×

The top curve of this "R" is too small and the diagonal leg much too long.

The letter "T" has been constructed with the pen at too steep an angle, which makes the horizontal strokes too heavy and the vertical ones too narrow.

T×

X×

The second stroke of the "X" crosses too high up the letter, and the serifs are too heavy.

GALLERY

This gallery section reflects the use of formal letter shapes in a variety of designs. Whether your choice of text is simple or more complex and depending upon your calligraphic expertise, a very sound understanding of basic letterforms is essential. You will then be able to explore new ideas. Using traditional layouts initially, then experimenting and gaining confidence to use your imagination, will help you to interpret a piece of text.

The sun was sinking. The hard stone of the day was cracked and light poured through its splinters. Red and gold shot through the waves, in rapid running arrows, feathered with darkness. Erratically rays of light flashed and wandered, like signals from sunken islands, or darts shot through laurel groves by shameless, laughing boys. But the waves, as they neared the shore, were robbed of light, and fell in one long concussion, like a wall falling, a wall of grey stone, unpierced by any chink of light. A breeze rose; a shiver ran through the leaves; and thus stirred they lost their brown density and became grey or white as the tree shifted its mass, winked, almost its domed uniformity. The hawk poised on the topmost branch flicked its eyelids and rose and sailed and soared far away. The wild plover cried in the marshes, evading, circling, and crying further off in the loneliness. The smoke of trains and chimneys was stretched and torn and became part of the fleecy canopy that hung over the sea and the fields. Now the corn was cut. Now only a brisk stubble was left of all its flowing and waving.

Slowly a great owl launched itself from the elm tree and swung and rose, as if on a line that dipped, to the height of the cedar. On the hills the slow shadows now broadened, now shrank, as they passed over. The pool on the top of the moor looked blank. No furry face looked there, or hoof splashed, or hot muzzle seethed in the water. A bird, perched on an ash-coloured twig, sipped a beak full of cold water. There was no sound of cropping, and no sound of wheels, but only the sudden roar of the wind letting its sails fill and brushing the tops of the grasses. One bone lay rain-pocked and sun-bleached till it shone like a twig that the sea has polished. The tree, that had burnt foxy-red in spring and in midsummer bent pliant leaves to the south wind, and was now black as iron, and as bare. The land was so distant that no shining roof or glittering window could be any longer seen. The tremendous weight of the shadowed earth had engulfed such frail fetters, such snail-shell encumbrances. Now there was only the liquid shadow of the cloud, the buffeting of the rain, a single darting spear of sunshine, or the sudden bruise of the rainstorm. Solitary trees marked distant hills like obelisks. From "The Waves" by Virginia Woolf.

Oh why ain't I blessed wiv green fingers
Why ain't me plants strong an' tall
How come all me neighbours reap fruits from their labours
While I never reaps 'bugger-all'?.

Me beetroots is pale an' anaemic
Me leeks grow no thicker than threads
Me cues an' tomaters is chronic non-starters
Cos me seeds never rise from their beds.

Me parsnips is parst orl redemption
Me peaches an' peas never crops
Me broad-beans an' marrers ain't fit for the sparrers
An' I'm buyin' me spuds up the shops.

I've giv'em orl kinds of perrection
I've tret'em like fammerly pets
Yet me bushes an' trees is beset wiv diseases
Wot nobody else never gets.

I works an' I waits an' I worries
I never 'as time ter relax
Me fingers is bleedin' from forkin' an' weedin'
While uvvers lie flat on their backs.

Me knuckles is covered in plasters
Me neck 'as a permanint crick
Me muscles is achin' from hoein' an' rakin'
An' me back ain't arf givin' me stick.

I've read every book in the libry
Consulted the experts by post
I've tried orl the capers described in the papers
An killed orf more plant life than most.

But I've never been known as a quitter
An' one day I'm gonna perfect
By intensive research down the ANGLER & PERCH
A garden that thrives on neglect.

◀ THE WAVES

Mary White has created a very well-controlled piece of writing in a slightly compressed roundhand style perfectly expressing the mood of the waves in a text by Virginia Woolf. Watercolor has played an important part in the overall effect, with gradual color changes throughout.

◀ THE FAILURE
William A. Hammond's presentation of this piece of Foundational hand lettering is most suitable for the text by J. J. Webster. The decorative initials representing vegetables are a charming addition and have been painted in gouache colors on Saunders Waterford HP paper.

I·WILL·ARISE·AND·GO·NOW, and go to Innisfree,
And a small cabin build there, of clay and wattles made:
Nine bean-rows will I have there, a hive for the honey-bee,
And live alone in the bee-loud glade.

AND·I·SHALL·HAVE·SOME·PEACE·THERE, for peace
comes dropping slow, dropping from the veils of the
morning to where the cricket sings;
There midnight's all a glimmer, and noon a purple glow,
And evening full of the linnet's wings.

I·WILL·ARISE·AND·GO·NOW, for always night and
day I hear lake water lapping with low sounds by the shore;
While I stand on the roadway, or on the pavements grey,
I hear it in the deep heart's core.

THE·LAKE·ISLE·OF·INNISFREE.   W.B.YEATS

▲ LAKE ISLE OF INNISFREE
A very pleasing traditional piece of writing using Foundational hand lower-case letters for the main body of the text by W. B. Yeats. Here Doreen Howley has used steel nibs with gouache colors on Fabriano Ingres paper. The top line of each verse has been written in Versal style lettering separated by tiny dots.

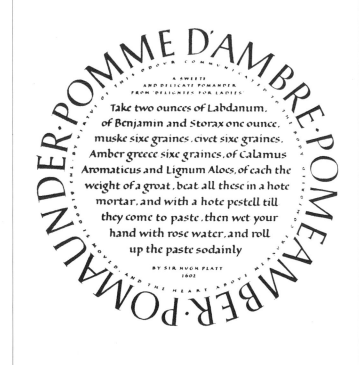

POMME D'AMBRE·POMEAMBER·POMAUNDER

· A SWEETE
AND DELICATE POMANDER
FROM 'DELIGHTES FOR LADIES'

Take two ounces of Labdanum,
of Benjamin and Storax one ounce,
muske sixe graines, civet sixe graines,
Amber greece sixe graines, of Calamus
Aromaticus and Lignum Aloes, of each the
weight of a groat, beat all these in a hote
mortar, and with a hote pestell till
they come to paste, then wet your
hand with rose water, and roll
up the paste sodainly

BY SIR HVGH PLATT
1602

◀ POMANDER
The combination of well-proportioned Versal letters written in a circle and a line of tiny capitals beneath is complemented by balanced Foundational hand lower-case letters in the center of the text. Lindsay Castell has used gouache color with quills on mold-made paper.

ITALIC SCRIPT

The Italic script developed in Renaissance Italy during the 15th century under such writing masters as Arrighi and Palantino. These humanist scribes wanted a less harsh minuscule than the Gothic style, which was difficult to read and write. They revived the rounder Carolingian style, developing a slightly more compressed and oval script with beautiful elongated ascenders and descenders. This allowed greater speed and fluency and, with fewer pen lifts, speeded up the copying of large amounts of text. The Italic scripts are probably the most useful everyday styles of writing used today.

MINUSCULE

Italic lower case, or minuscule, where the pen is held at a steeper 45° angle, allows the calligrapher to write at a greater speed. This alphabet is made up of oval shapes and serifs, and springing arches and is written at a gentle forward slope. It can be easily adjusted to different weights and sizes and has great flexibility in the length of the ascenders and descenders, allowing them to be flourished.

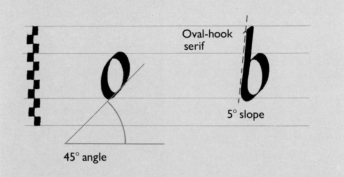

ESSENTIAL INFORMATION

Oval-hook serif

45° angle

5° slope

Letter height The x height is 5 nib widths, with the ascenders and descenders extending an extra 3 nib widths each.

Basic pen angle The pen angle between the nib and the writing line is 45°. A shallower 20° angle is used for crossbars.

"O" form An oval-shaped "o" is used here.

Slope Letters may slant forward between 5° and 10° from the vertical, but a 5° slant is enough for a more formal Italic.

Serif forms Small oval-hook serifs echoing the oval "o" are most suitable for this alphabet.

GEOMETRIC FORMS

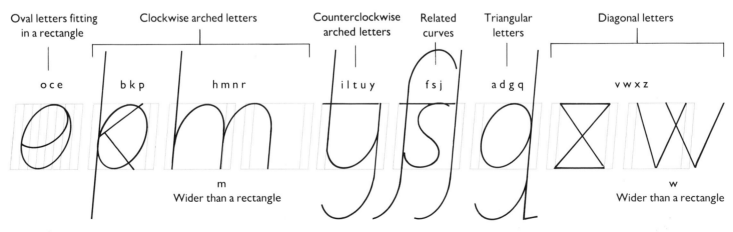

Oval letters fitting in a rectangle — o c e

Clockwise arched letters — b k p   h m n r

Counterclockwise arched letters — i l t u y

Related curves — f s j

Triangular letters — a d g q

Diagonal letters — v w x z

m
Wider than a rectangle

w
Wider than a rectangle

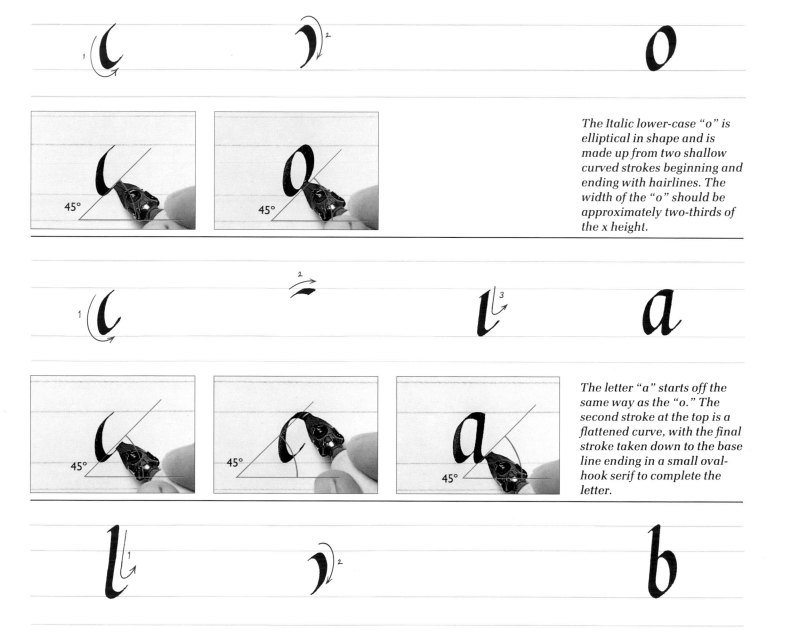

The Italic lower-case "o" is elliptical in shape and is made up from two shallow curved strokes beginning and ending with hairlines. The width of the "o" should be approximately two-thirds of the x height.

The letter "a" starts off the same way as the "o." The second stroke at the top is a flattened curve, with the final stroke taken down to the base line ending in a small oval-hook serif to complete the letter.

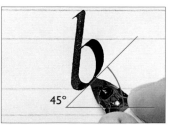

The lower-case Italic letter "b" starts with a small oval-hook serif at the top of the ascender line moving down toward the base line, but curving upward just before reaching it. The second stroke is the same as the right-hand curve of the letter "o," but this time touches the stem of the letter at the hairline.

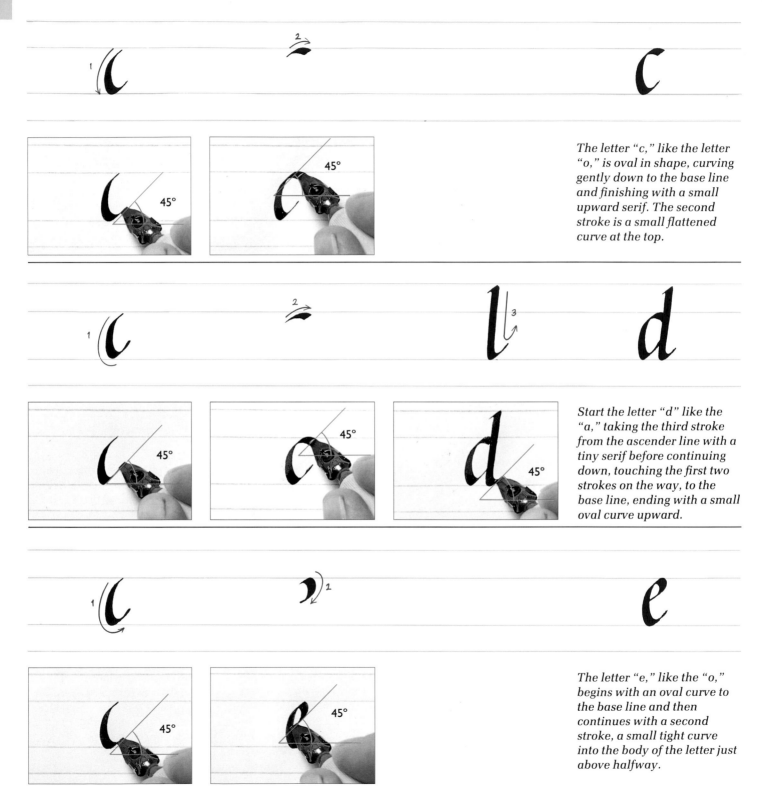

The letter "c," like the letter "o," is oval in shape, curving gently down to the base line and finishing with a small upward serif. The second stroke is a small flattened curve at the top.

Start the letter "d" like the "a," taking the third stroke from the ascender line with a tiny serif before continuing down, touching the first two strokes on the way, to the base line, ending with a small oval curve upward.

The letter "e," like the "o," begins with an oval curve to the base line and then continues with a second stroke, a small tight curve into the body of the letter just above halfway.

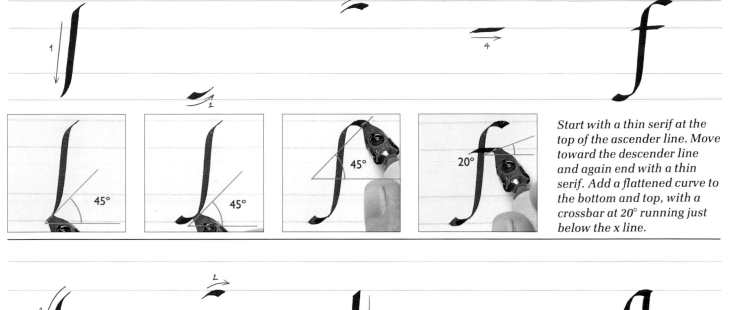

Start with a thin serif at the top of the ascender line. Move toward the descender line and again end with a thin serif. Add a flattened curve to the bottom and top, with a crossbar at 20° running just below the x line.

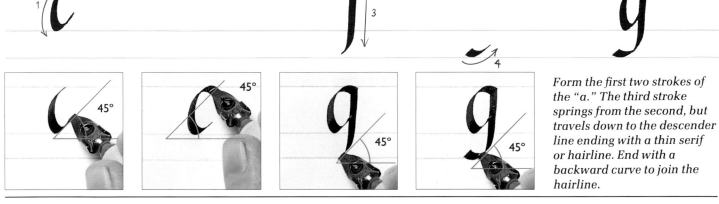

Form the first two strokes of the "a." The third stroke springs from the second, but travels down to the descender line ending with a thin serif or hairline. End with a backward curve to join the hairline.

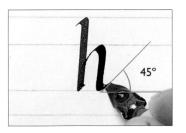

The letter "h" starts with a small oval-hook serif at the ascender line before proceeding downward at a 5° slant to the base line, again ending with a small serif. The second stroke, like the letter "n," springs from the base of the stem, leaving it just above halfway before arching over and down to the base line. Add a curved serif to complete the letter.

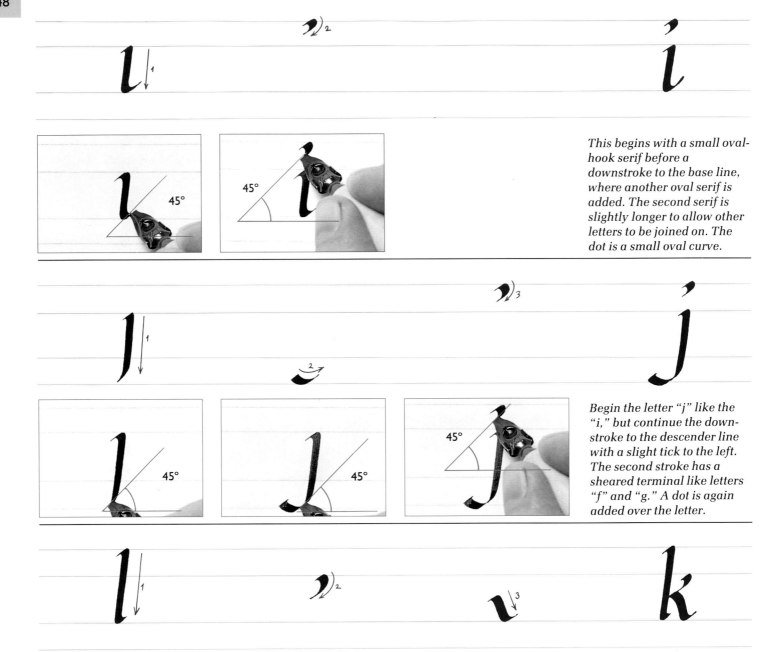

This begins with a small oval-hook serif before a downstroke to the base line, where another oval serif is added. The second serif is slightly longer to allow other letters to be joined on. The dot is a small oval curve.

Begin the letter "j" like the "i," but continue the down-stroke to the descender line with a slight tick to the left. The second stroke has a sheared terminal like letters "f" and "g." A dot is again added over the letter.

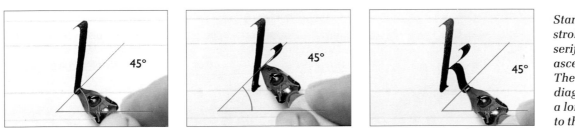

Start and finish the first stroke with a small oval-hook serif from the top of the ascender line to the base line. The second stroke curves diagonally into the stem, with a longer diagonal continuing to the base line.

This has only one stroke, which starts at the ascender line with a small oval-hook serif descending at 5° to the vertical down to the base line. From here curve upward, but be careful not to curve too much or too soon.

The downstroke starts and ends with a small oval-hook serif. From the base of their stems, arch two strokes from just above halfway to return to the base line. Add oval serifs, slightly longer on the third stroke.

Start and finish the first stroke with a small oval-hook serif. The second stroke springs from the base of the letter body, leaving it just above halfway, arching and then moving to the base line before curving up gently.

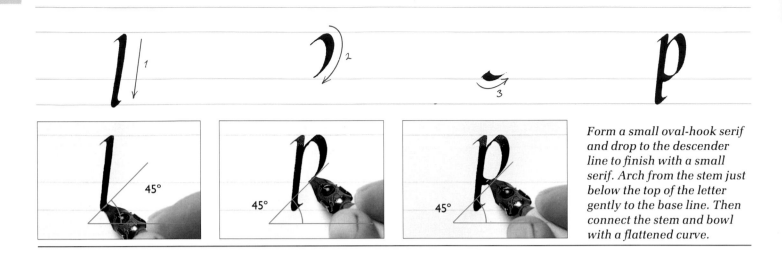

Form a small oval-hook serif and drop to the descender line to finish with a small serif. Arch from the stem just below the top of the letter gently to the base line. Then connect the stem and bowl with a flattened curve.

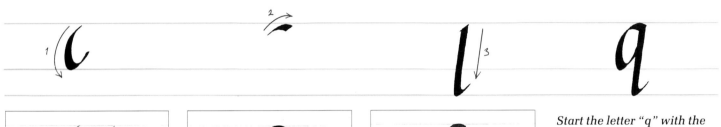

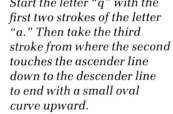

Start the letter "q" with the first two strokes of the letter "a." Then take the third stroke from where the second touches the ascender line down to the descender line to end with a small oval curve upward.

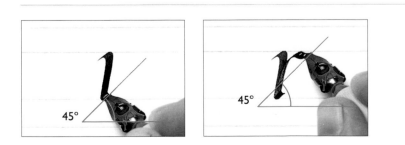

The lower-case "r" starts on the x line with a small oval serif and goes down to the base line to finish with another small serif. The second stroke branches like the "n" out of the stem, but then gently curves upward.

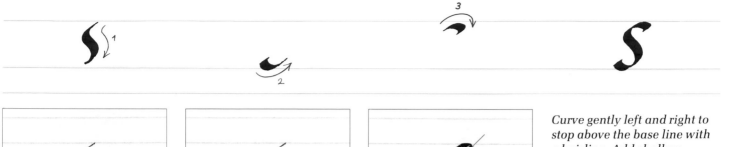

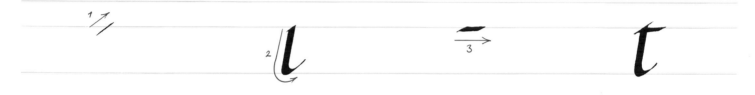

Curve gently left and right to stop above the base line with a hairline. Add shallow curves joining the letter top and bottom. Make the top counter slightly smaller; the letter should align at the right with a 5° slant.

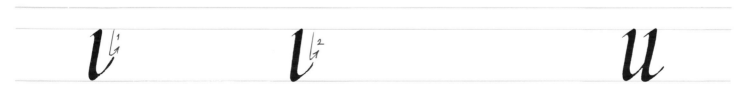

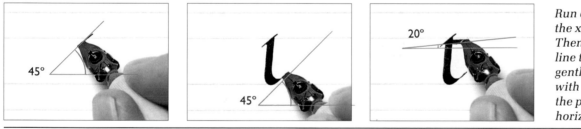

Run a thin diagonal through the x line to form the serif. Then go from the top of the x line to the base line and gently curve upward. Finish with a lilting crossbar, with the pen at 20° to the horizontal, below the x line.

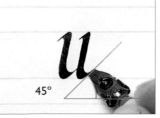

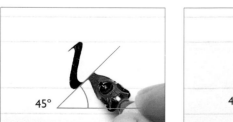

The letter "u" mirrors the letter "n": two strokes starting with small oval-hook serifs proceeding down to the base line before curving up at the end. The second stroke connects to the first at the end of the curve.

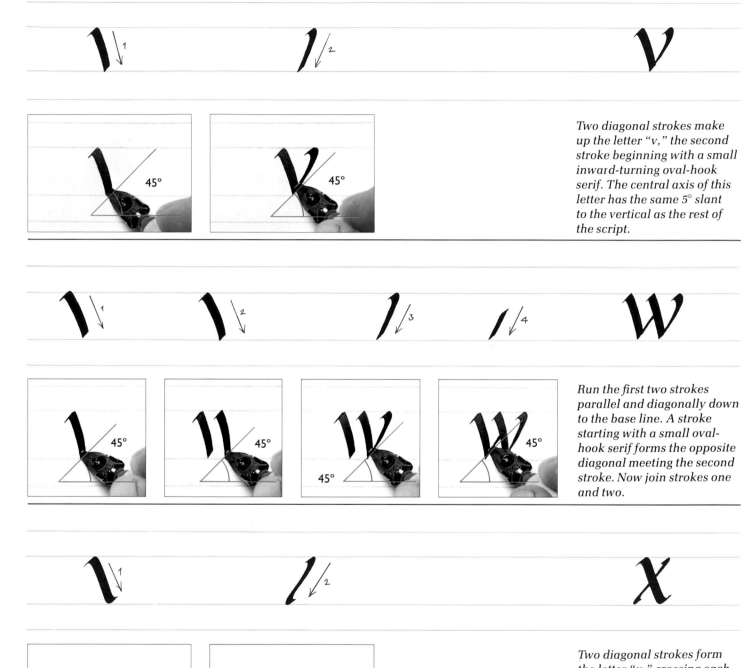

Two diagonal strokes make up the letter "v," the second stroke beginning with a small inward-turning oval-hook serif. The central axis of this letter has the same 5° slant to the vertical as the rest of the script.

Run the first two strokes parallel and diagonally down to the base line. A stroke starting with a small oval-hook serif forms the opposite diagonal meeting the second stroke. Now join strokes one and two.

Two diagonal strokes form the letter "x," crossing each other just above the center. The second diagonal starts and ends with a very small oval-hook serif.

The first stroke of the letter "y" begins like the letter "u," but the second continues down to a hairline just above the descender line. The third stroke is a flattened curve joining the letter at the hairline.

First form the top horizontal line. The second stroke is a diagonal line which tapers at both ends from and into the horizontal strokes. The lower horizontal has a more exaggerated tapering serif.

ALTERNATIVES

There are a number of alternative lower-case letters with various serifs, allowing greater flexibility within this alphabet, particularly with the flourishing of letters.

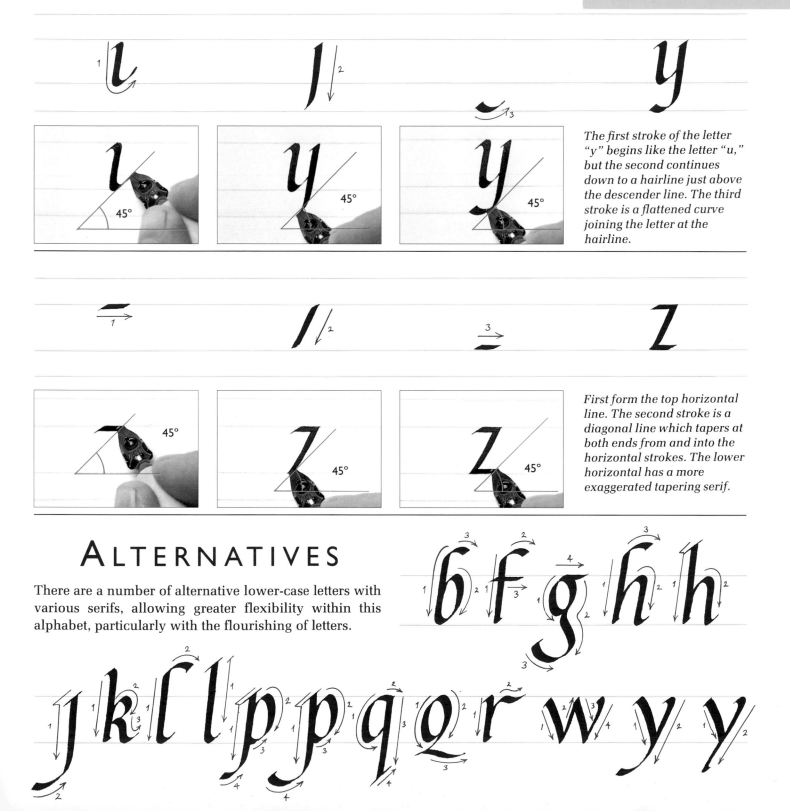

TROUBLESHOOTING

As this alphabet can be written at greater speed, special attention should be given to the consistency of the slope. So make sure all the letters are at the same angle and not some upright and some slanting. Watch out for the inner bowl of the letter "e," which should not be too small or it will look as if it is closing up and might even resemble the letter "c," making the script difficult to read. Try to keep characteristics of the alphabet consistent, such as springing arches on letters "n," "m," and "u," and the crossbars of "f" and "t," which should not be too heavy.

The crossbar of the letter "f" has been formed at too flat an angle, making it too heavy.

CORRECT LETTERFORMS

abcdefghijklm

The first oval curve of the letter "a" does not continue high enough up, making it too rounded.

The top of the letter "c" is too curved down, a mistake which gives the letter a hooked appearance.

The top curve of the letter "k" is far too small and the diagonal tail too long.

The top curve into the body of the letter "e" is far too small, closing up the counter space.

The top curve of this example of the letter "k" is too large and the diagonal leg, therefore, far too short.

The top curve into the body of this "e" is too big, creating too much counter space.

The top curve of the letter "s" has been constructed too small and the bottom curve too big; the letter looks as if it is falling over.

s ×

The pen angle has been held too flat, making this letter heavier than usual.

v ×

n o p q r s t u v w x y z

p ×

The point where the bottom of the oval joins the stem has been constructed too high up the letter, which makes it look heavy.

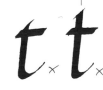

t × *t* ×

The top of the letter "t" is too tall and the crossbar too heavy.

The crossbar of this "t" is too heavy.

z ×

The pen has been held at too steep an angle for the diagonal stroke, so it is too thin.

CAPITALS

Italic capitals are based on compressed Roman capitals which appear oval in shape. They have small oval serifs and, like the lower case letters, have great flexibility in height and weight, making them suitable for headings or entire pieces of text. This alphabet also lends itself to flourishes, adding great grace and beauty to the letters.

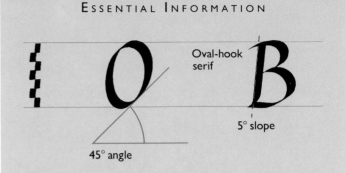

ESSENTIAL INFORMATION

Oval-hook serif

45° angle

5° slope

Letter height The height here is 7 nib widths, but the letters can be written at a taller 8 nib widths.
Basic pen angle The pen is usually held at a 45° angle.
"O" form Oval.
Slope Letters may slant forward between 5° and 10°.
Serif forms Small oval-hook serifs should be used.

GEOMETRIC FORMS

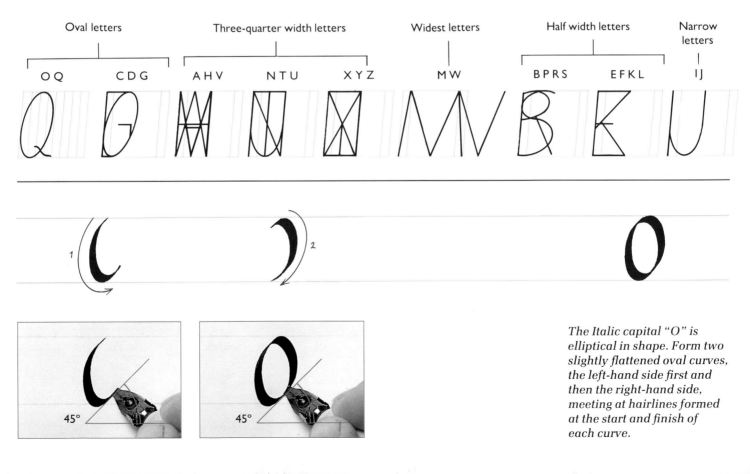

Oval letters	Three-quarter width letters	Widest letters	Half width letters	Narrow letters
O Q C D G	A H V N T U X Y Z	M W	B P R S E F K L	I J

The Italic capital "O" is elliptical in shape. Form two slightly flattened oval curves, the left-hand side first and then the right-hand side, meeting at hairlines formed at the start and finish of each curve.

45°

45°

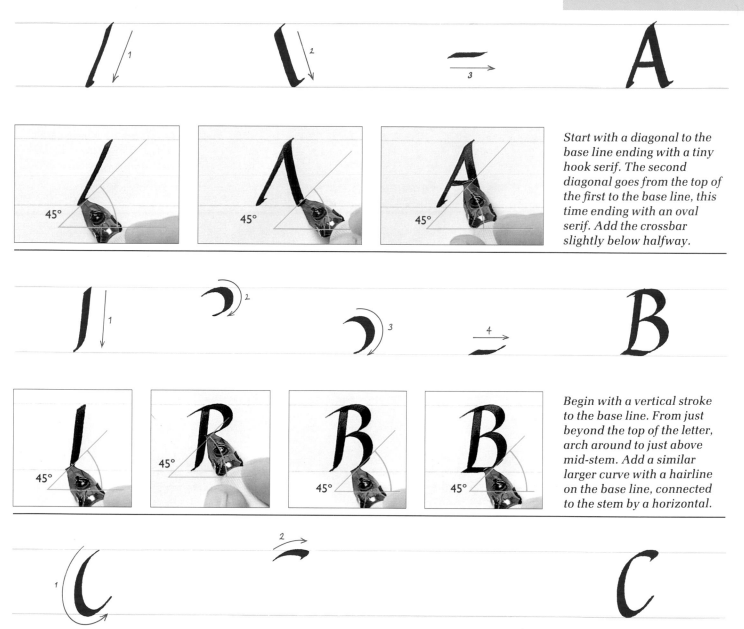

Start with a diagonal to the base line ending with a tiny hook serif. The second diagonal goes from the top of the first to the base line, this time ending with an oval serif. Add the crossbar slightly below halfway.

Begin with a vertical stroke to the base line. From just beyond the top of the letter, arch around to just above mid-stem. Add a similar larger curve with a hairline on the base line, connected to the stem by a horizontal.

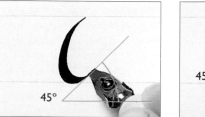
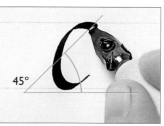

The first stroke of the letter "C" is the same as that for the letter "O": an oval curve from the top of the cap line to the base line ending with an upward curve. The second stroke, a flattened curve, forms the head of the letter.

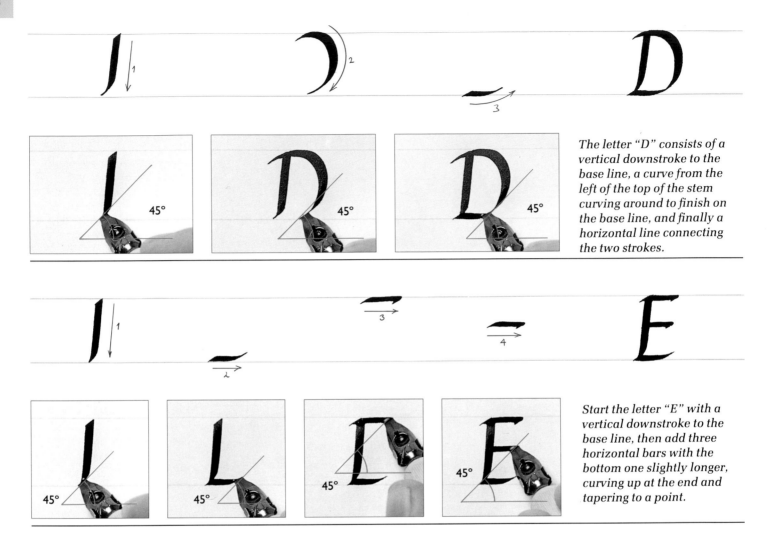

The letter "D" consists of a vertical downstroke to the base line, a curve from the left of the top of the stem curving around to finish on the base line, and finally a horizontal line connecting the two strokes.

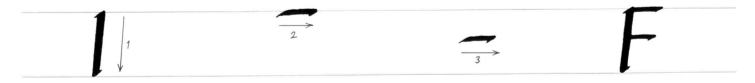

Start the letter "E" with a vertical downstroke to the base line, then add three horizontal bars with the bottom one slightly longer, curving up at the end and tapering to a point.

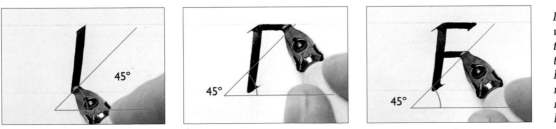

Like the "E," the "F" starts with a vertical downstroke to the base line, ending with a tiny oval-hook serif. Add horizontal bars to the top and middle of the stem. The middle arm should be halfway or slightly below.

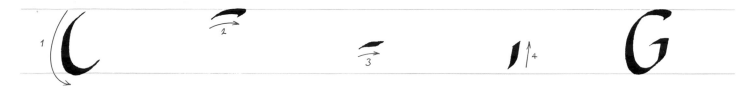

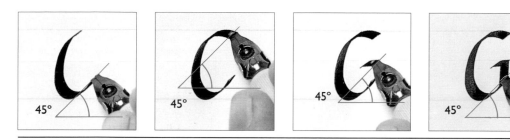

The first two strokes of the letter "G" are like those of "C." Then add a small horizontal line on the right and continue with a vertical stroke joining the hairline ending of the first stroke.

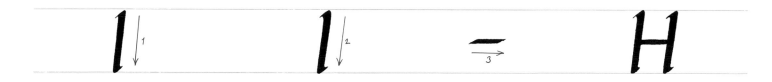

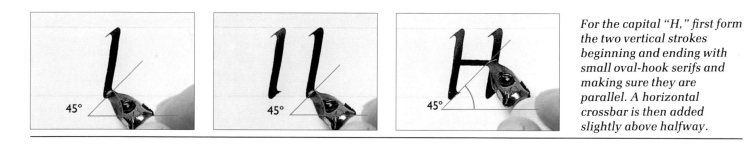

For the capital "H," first form the two vertical strokes beginning and ending with small oval-hook serifs and making sure they are parallel. A horizontal crossbar is then added slightly above halfway.

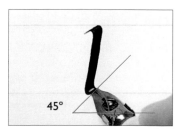

Make a small oval serif at the top of the "I," continuing the vertical downstroke down to the base line. Finish the stroke with another small oval serif.

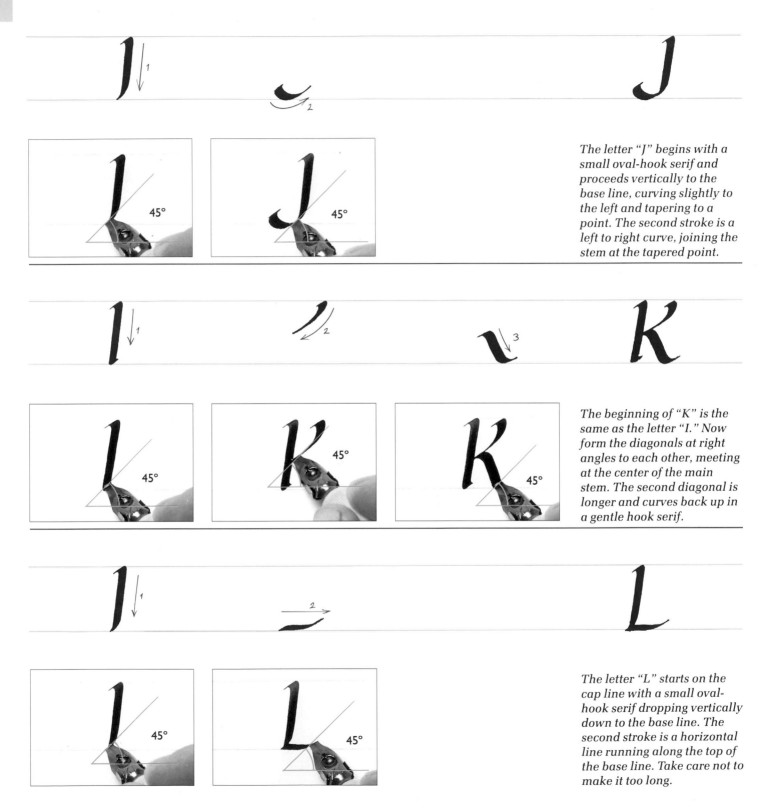

The letter "J" begins with a small oval-hook serif and proceeds vertically to the base line, curving slightly to the left and tapering to a point. The second stroke is a left to right curve, joining the stem at the tapered point.

The beginning of "K" is the same as the letter "I." Now form the diagonals at right angles to each other, meeting at the center of the main stem. The second diagonal is longer and curves back up in a gentle hook serif.

The letter "L" starts on the cap line with a small oval-hook serif dropping vertically down to the base line. The second stroke is a horizontal line running along the top of the base line. Take care not to make it too long.

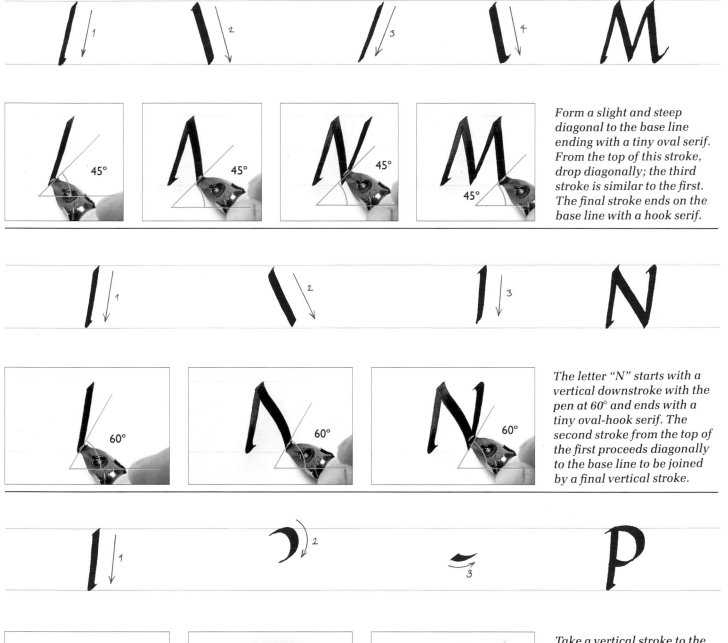

Form a slight and steep diagonal to the base line ending with a tiny oval serif. From the top of this stroke, drop diagonally; the third stroke is similar to the first. The final stroke ends on the base line with a hook serif.

The letter "N" starts with a vertical downstroke with the pen at 60° and ends with a tiny oval-hook serif. The second stroke from the top of the first proceeds diagonally to the base line to be joined by a final vertical stroke.

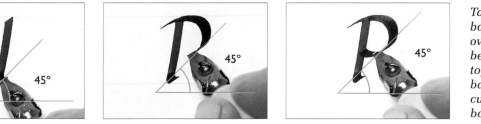

Take a vertical stroke to the base line ending with a tiny oval serif. The second stroke begins just to the left of the top of the stem, curving down back toward it. A shallow curve joins the stem in the bowl.

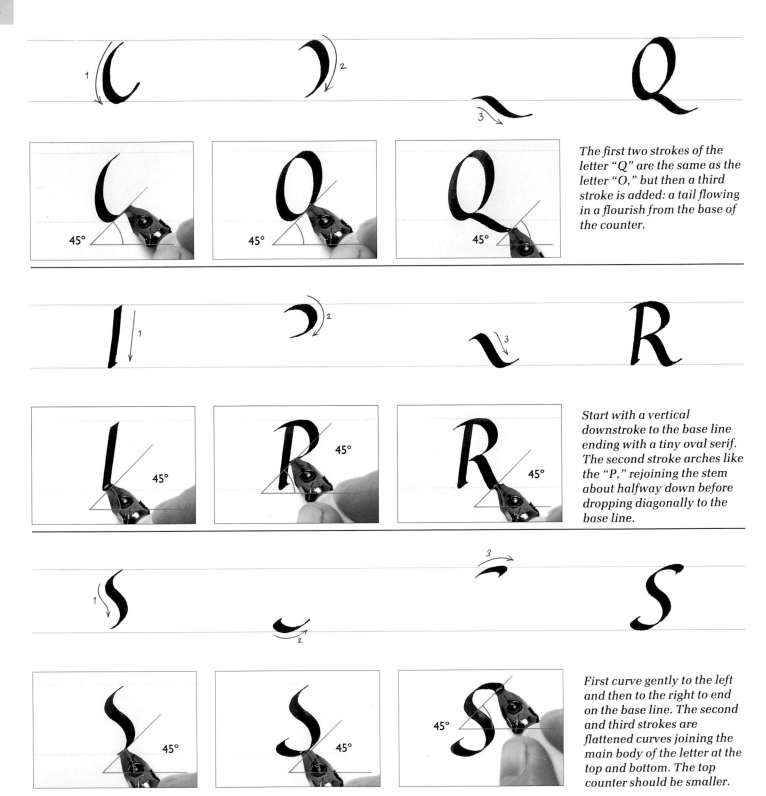

The first two strokes of the letter "Q" are the same as the letter "O," but then a third stroke is added: a tail flowing in a flourish from the base of the counter.

Start with a vertical downstroke to the base line ending with a tiny oval serif. The second stroke arches like the "P," rejoining the stem about halfway down before dropping diagonally to the base line.

First curve gently to the left and then to the right to end on the base line. The second and third strokes are flattened curves joining the main body of the letter at the top and bottom. The top counter should be smaller.

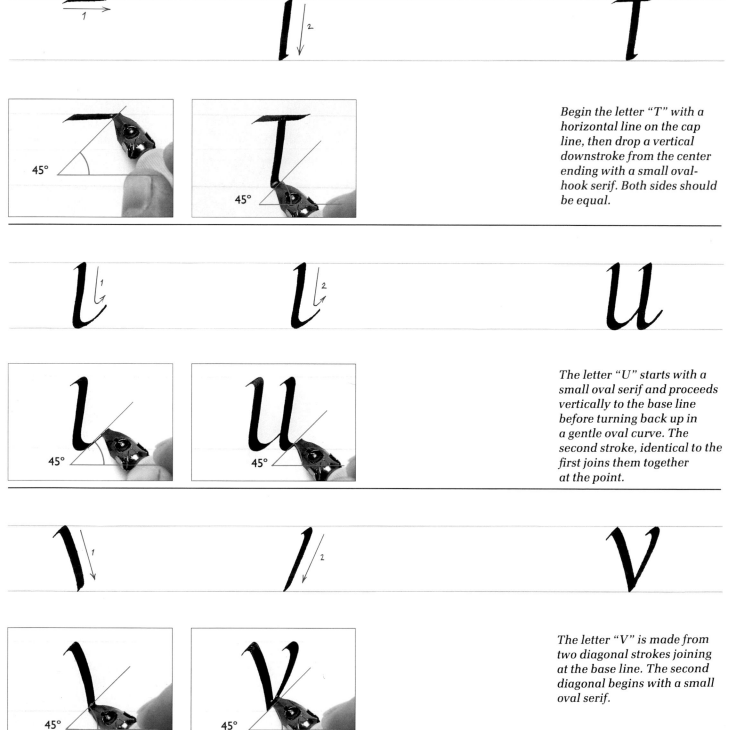

Begin the letter "T" with a horizontal line on the cap line, then drop a vertical downstroke from the center ending with a small oval-hook serif. Both sides should be equal.

The letter "U" starts with a small oval serif and proceeds vertically to the base line before turning back up in a gentle oval curve. The second stroke, identical to the first joins them together at the point.

The letter "V" is made from two diagonal strokes joining at the base line. The second diagonal begins with a small oval serif.

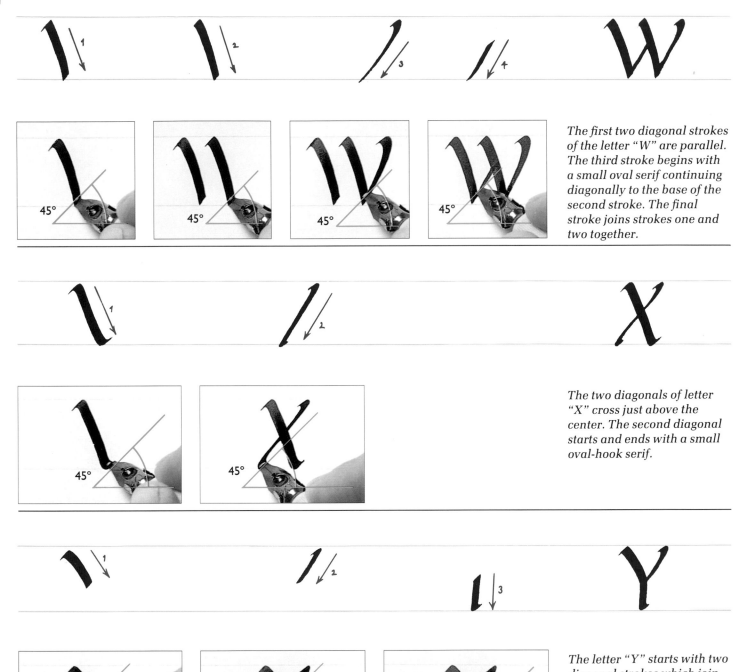

The first two diagonal strokes of the letter "W" are parallel. The third stroke begins with a small oval serif continuing diagonally to the base of the second stroke. The final stroke joins strokes one and two together.

The two diagonals of letter "X" cross just above the center. The second diagonal starts and ends with a small oval-hook serif.

The letter "Y" starts with two diagonal strokes which join in the middle of the capital height. The third stroke then continues vertically down to the base line, ending with a tiny oval serif.

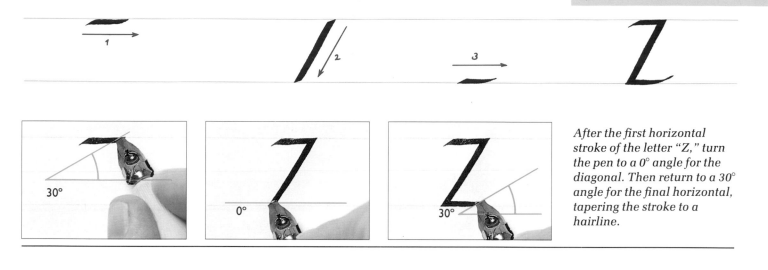

After the first horizontal stroke of the letter "Z," turn the pen to a 0° angle for the diagonal. Then return to a 30° angle for the final horizontal, tapering the stroke to a hairline.

ALTERNATIVES

With the rhythm of this capital alphabet, there are many possibilities for alternative letters and flourishes. The punctuation and numbers follow the shape and angle of the oval form, and the numbers can either align with the capital height or with the smaller lower case.

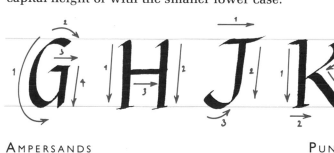

AMPERSANDS

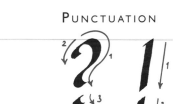

PUNCTUATION

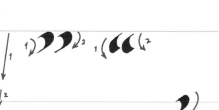

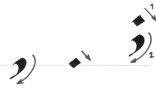

NUMERALS

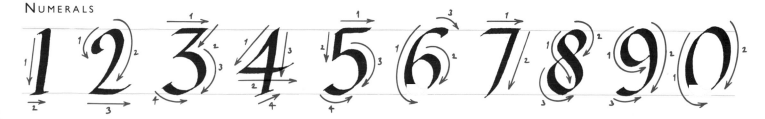

TROUBLESHOOTING

As Italic capitals are based on an oval shape, special care should be taken to keep this oval consistent. Pay special attention to letters such as the "A" and "H," which should not be too wide. Take care, too, with horizontal strokes in letters such as "E," "F," "L," "T" and "Z," making sure that they are not too heavy, too long or too wavy.

The vertical stems of the letter "H" have been constructed too far apart, and the crossbar is too high.

The horizontal line at the bottom of the letter "L" is far too long.

CORRECT LETTERFORMS

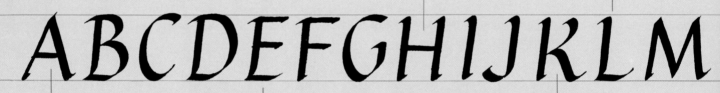

ABCDEFGHIJKLM

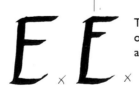

The letter "A" is splayed out too wide, giving it a collapsed appearance; the crossbar is also too high.

The top horizontal arm of the letter "E" is far too long and the middle arm too short, making the letter look as if it is falling over.

The middle horizontal arm of this "E" is too small and too high up the stem.

The first diagonal curve of the letter "K" is too long, therefore making the bottom diagonal much too short.

The diagonal strokes of the letter "X" cross each other too high up the letter, making the lower part too wide and the top too small.

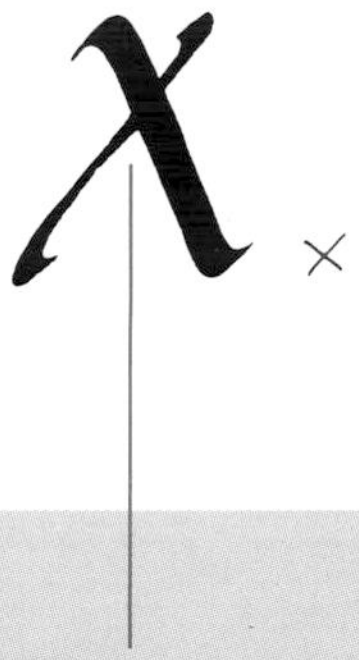

The curve at the top of the letter "R" is too small, making the diagonal tail much too long.

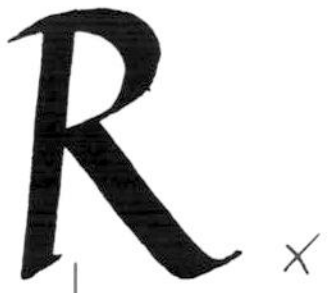

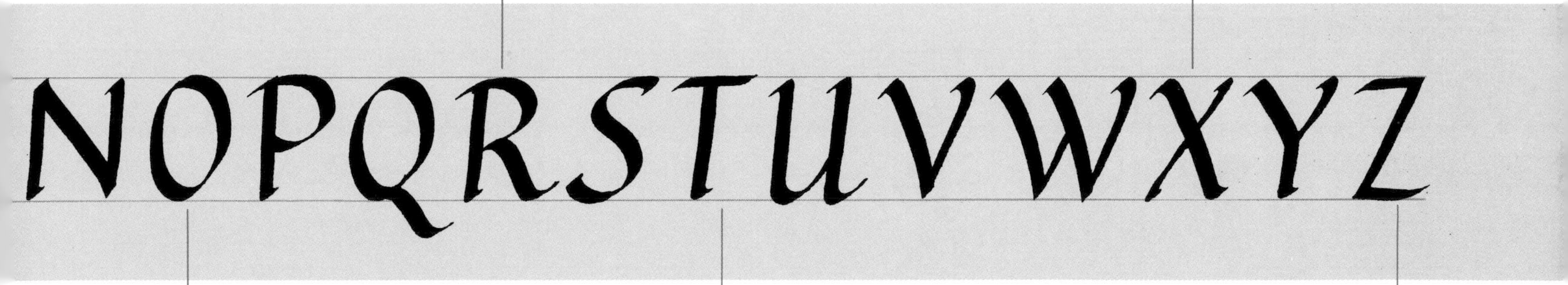

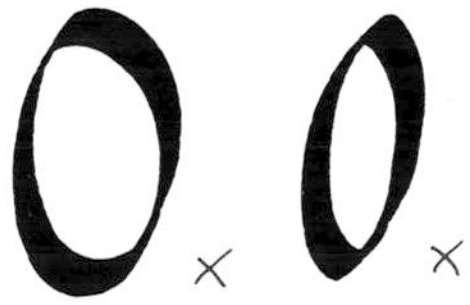

R

X

NOPQRSTUVWXYZ

O O

The letter "O" is much too narrow and is not consistent with this alphabet.

The first curve of this "O" continues too far around at the base of the letter, which makes the letter appear as if it is falling over.

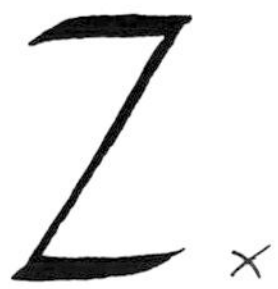

Z

The diagonal stroke of the letter "Z" is far too thin as the pen has been held at too steep an angle.

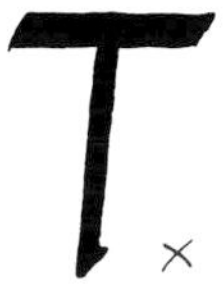

T

The horizontal line of the letter "T" is far too heavy and thick and does not tie in with the rest of the alphabet.

GALLERY

The lettering shown in this gallery introduces the use of capital letters in a formal design, and continues with a very well-controlled use of color and creativity. For calligraphers at all levels of expertise, capital letters need a great deal of practice, but the result is well worth working for. Letterforms including decoration and color can enhance a piece of text in a variety of ways. Exploring new ideas and mastering pen control increases confidence, allowing you to experiment and create beautiful artwork.

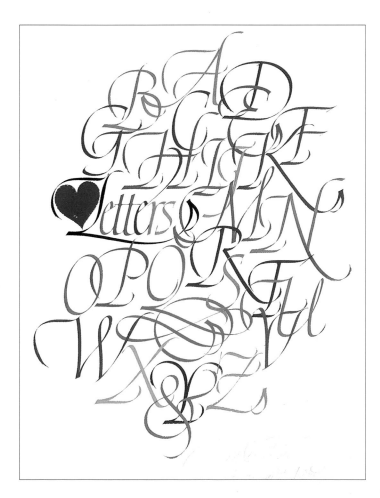

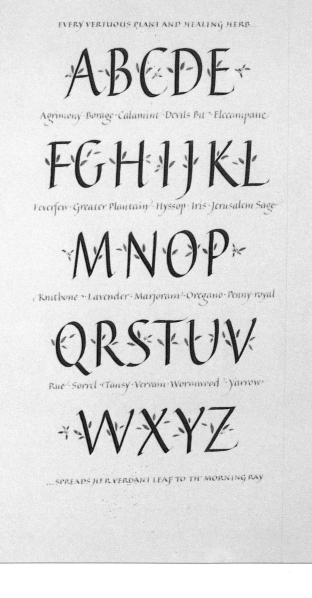

◀ ALPHABET DESIGN

This beautifully designed calligraphic alphabet using capital letters with superb flourishes shows that Jean Larcher has achieved tremendous control and flexibility of design and layout. Multicolors have been used throughout, with a red heart positioned perfectly against the letter "L." Colored lowercase letters make up the word "Letters."

◄ HERBAL ALPHABET
This excellent example of very well-written Italic capital letters using the whole alphabet shows calligrapher Lindsay Castell to have great skill and control. The capital letters are complemented by the very small Italic Cursive lower-case letters with the names of herbs using all letters of the alphabet. The decoration used around the capitals has been made with a rubber stamp design and brush. This work, written on mold-made paper using metal nibs and gouache colors, was inspired by the healing properties of herbs and herb gardens.

► WALDEN POND
Jenny Hunter Groat has written the main text of this poem by Henry David Thoreau in flowing Italic lower-case letters with extremely well-controlled flourishes, particularly in the last word which incorporates the very well-positioned name of the author and title. The butterfly at the top of the page has been drawn very freely to give the feeling of great movement across the page, leading perfectly into the top three lines of well-balanced capital letters.

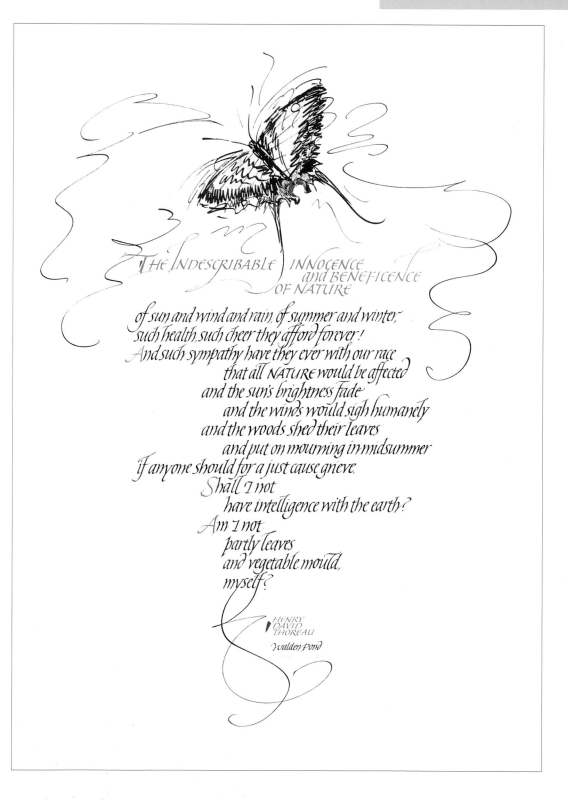

THE INDESCRIBABLE INNOCENCE and BENEFICENCE OF NATURE

of sun and wind and rain, of summer and winter,
such health, such cheer they afford forever!
And such sympathy have they ever with our race
that all NATURE would be affected
and the sun's brightness fade
and the winds would sigh humanely
and the woods shed their leaves
and put on mourning in midsummer
if anyone should for a just cause grieve.
Shall I not
have intelligence with the earth?
Am I not
partly leaves
and vegetable mould,
myself?

HENRY DAVID THOREAU
Walden Pond

▶ THE FISH

A well-designed piece of Italic lettering has been used by Janet Mehigan for Rupert Brooke's The Fish using gouache in tones of blue on India handmade paper. The gold bubbles that appear on the left-hand side of the work have been painted with gum ammoniac size and then transfer leaf applied.

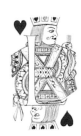

▲ THE RAPE OF THE LOCK

Designing a manuscript book is quite different from working on individual sheets, as balancing the layout of the text, margins and illustrations all need to be taken into account. The comic epic poem by Alexander Pope is reflected in the choice of Italic lettering, together with the illustration in the form of images of a card game. Polly Morris has used metal pens, watercolor, gouache and shell gold on Zerkall paper.

The Fish

In a cool curving world he lies
And ripples with dark ecstasies
The kind luxurious lapse and steal
Shapes all his universe to feel
And know and be; the clinging stream
Closes his memory, glooms his dream
Who lips the roots o' the shore and glides
Superb on unreturning tides
Those silent waters weave for him
A fluctuant mutable world and dim
Where wavering masses bulge and gape
Mysterious, and shape to shape
Dies momently through whorl and hollow
And form and line and solid follow
Solid and line and form to dream
Fantastic down the eternal stream
An obscure world, a shifting world
Bulbous, or pulled to thin or curled
Or serpentine or driving arrows
Or serene slidings or March narrows
There shipping wave and shore are one
And weed and mud. No ray of sun
But glow to glow fades down the deep
As dream to unknown dream in sleep
Shaken translucency illumes
The hyaline of drifting glooms
The strange soft-handed depth subdues
Drowned colour there, but black to hues
As death to living, decomposes
Red darkness of the heart of roses
Blue brilliant from dead starless skies
And gold that lies behind the eyes
The unknown unnameable sightless white
That is the essential flame of night
Lustreless purple, hooded green
The myriad hues that lie between
Darkness and darkness!... And all's one
Gentle, embracing, quiet, dun
The world he rests in, the world he knows
Perpetual curving, Only — grows
An eddy in that ordered falling
A knowledge from the gloom, a calling
Weed in wave, gleam in the mud —
The dark fire leaps along his blood
Dateless and deathless, blind and still
The intricate impulse works its will
His woven world drops back and he
Sans providence, sans memory
Unconscious and directly driven
Fades to some dank sufficient heaven

FROM THE FISH BY RUPERT BROOKE

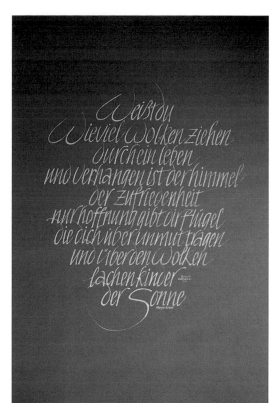

▲ WOLKEN
Here Mary White has used a quill and white watercolor to recreate Margot Brust's modern German poem Clouds. This approach gives the Italic lower-case lettering a pointed feel balanced by the more rounded capitals and very fine hairlines.

▼ CEDAR WAXWINGS
This piece of calligraphy has been written with both a metal pen and a quill pen and was designed to be printed. A good contrast of Italic styles has been utilized by Jenny Hunter Groat, beginning with a very formal style proceeding to freely written capitals and continuing with a very tall compressed Italic cursive style.

Our hillside was so steep that the small deck outside our living-room window was high in the trees. The area is a breeding and migratory canyon for birds and many different kinds visited us each year.

One autumn morning I awoke to see the air, trees and deck filled with thousands of cedar waxwings feeding on fruit from the masses of grape ivy hanging from the redwoods, oaks and bays. There were so many birds that not only did they crowd the rim of the large flower-pot saucer which held their drinking water, but stood on each other's backs in the water itself. Their flutter and chatter were incessant. As I tried to photograph them I realized that I was able to approach very near them at the sliding door.

Suddenly a California Brush Jay screeched into the feeding area and the deck was temporarily cleared. On a hunch, I crept out onto the deck, pulled the water dish very close to me, and sat down in meditation posture, extending my hands to rest on my knees, fingers made into perches. With eyes nearly closed and breathing imperceptible, I waited. Before long a bold Mountain Chickadee looked me over, then came to drink, only inches away. Seeing him, the waxwings, too, began to return and, FOR THE NEXT TEN MINUTES I WAS COVERED WITH BIRDS. They filled the dish, splattering me with water all over. They clung to my brown homespun sweater, landed on my head, nose and toes, and held the fingers of both hands into them; this was all over my toes, my knees and everywhere. At last, in sheer delight, I caught my breath, and they fled.

▼ Das Brot

Mary White has used a very individual style of Italic lettering for this German quotation Bread. Written in pen, ink and watercolor, it shows great confidence and pen control. The large, freely written heading balances the work perfectly.

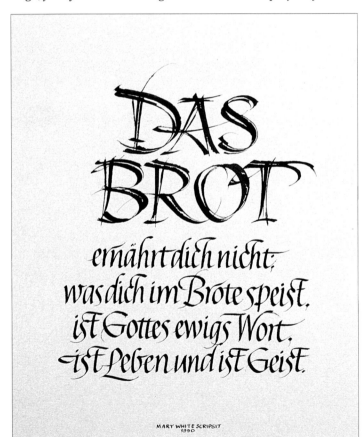

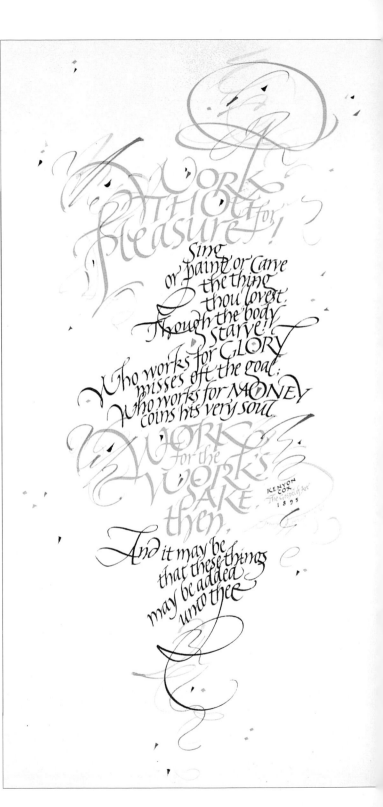

◀ WORK THOU FOR PLEASURE
This exciting and free-flowing piece of lettering gives the feeling of dancing on the page. Written by Jenny Hunter Groat with various sizes of quills in ink, this quotation is from The Gospel of Art *by Kenyon Cox. Wonderfully controlled flourishes have been added to give the work a very lively feel to it, particularly the title. Extra ornamentation in several colors has been added using a brush.*

▶ HE REACHED Q
This text is an extract from Virginia Woolf's To the Lighthouse *written by Annie Moring in various sizes of Italic, including capitals with raised gold dots in between. The large letter "Q" has been written with a piece of balsa wood using gum ammoniac, gesso and then burnished gold leaf on Saunders Waterford HP paper.*

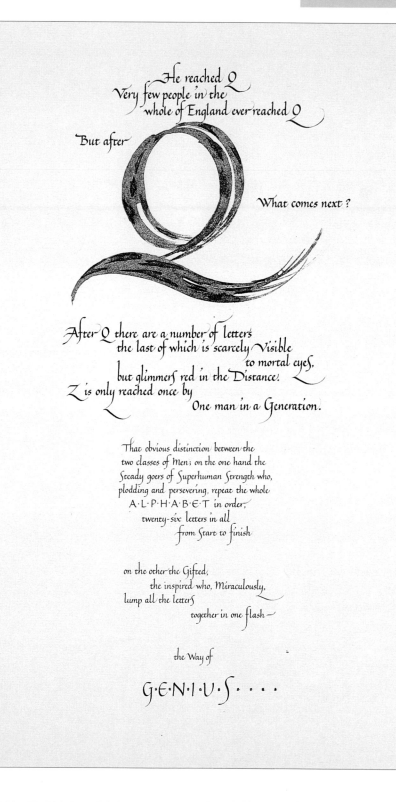

He reached Q
Very few people in the
whole of England ever reached Q
But after
What comes next?

After Q there are a number of letters
the last of which is scarcely visible
to mortal eyes,
but glimmers red in the Distance.
Z is only reached once by
One man in a Generation.

That obvious distinction between the
two classes of Men; on the one hand the
Steady goers of Superhuman Strength who,
plodding and persevering, repeat the whole
A·L·P·H·A·B·E·T in order,
twenty-six letters in all
from Start to finish

on the other the Gifted,
the inspired who, Miraculously,
lump all the letters
together in one flash ~

the Way of
G·E·N·I·U·S····

ROMAN CAPITALS

The Roman letterform was based on the Greek and evolved over hundreds of years. Classical examples of Roman capitals are mostly found incised in stone or marble, recording important events. Scribes painted these large beautiful letters with reed brushes onto the stone, and then the stonecutters would chisel (or cut) the capitals into the stone. Such inscriptions reached a height of perfection with the Trajan column inscription toward the end of the first century.

The pen was also used to write such capitals or "majuscules": first came reed pens, followed by quills. Today a metal broad-edged or square-ended pen is used which, when held at various angles, can achieve the thick and thin strokes of this elegant letterform.

Roman square capitals or *quadrata* are constructed according to geometric principles, using a circle, square and proportions of them. Careful control of the pen will allow the calligrapher to achieve the basic 30° pen angle with small hook serifs beginning the letters. A more difficult, very flat 0° angle slab serif is required for the lower serifs. Well-proportioned letters and even spacing will lead to an understanding of all other letterforms.

ESSENTIAL INFORMATION

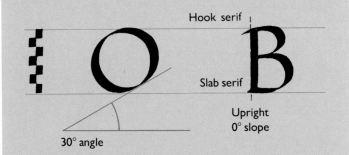

Hook serif

Slab serif

Upright
0° slope

30° angle

Letter height The height here is 7 nib widths.
Basic pen angle The pen angle for most letters is 30°. However, for diagonal strokes the angle is steeper at 45° and steeper still for thin diagonals, at 60°. For horizontal crossbars a flatter angle of 20° is used.
Slope This is an upright alphabet with the letters constructed vertical to the writing line.
Serif forms Small hook serifs are added at the top of the letters, and slab serifs at the bottom of the letters. If gaps appear, fill them in with the edge of the nib.

GEOMETRIC FORMS

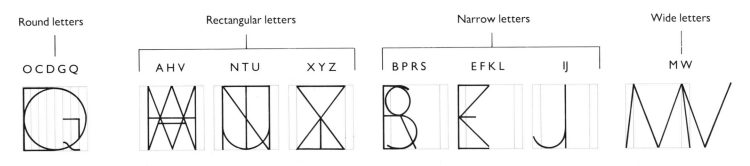

Round letters

OCDGQ

Rectangular letters

AHV   NTU   XYZ

Narrow letters

BPRS   EFKL   IJ

Wide letters

MW

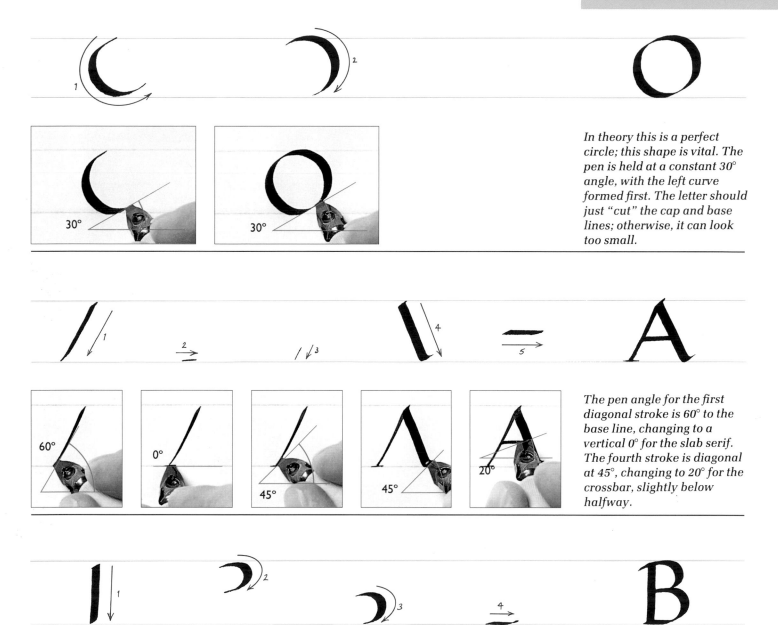

In theory this is a perfect circle; this shape is vital. The pen is held at a constant 30° angle, with the left curve formed first. The letter should just "cut" the cap and base lines; otherwise, it can look too small.

The pen angle for the first diagonal stroke is 60° to the base line, changing to a vertical 0° for the slab serif. The fourth stroke is diagonal at 45°, changing to 20° for the crossbar, slightly below halfway.

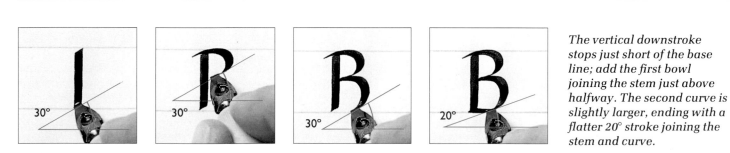

The vertical downstroke stops just short of the base line; add the first bowl joining the stem just above halfway. The second curve is slightly larger, ending with a flatter 20° stroke joining the stem and curve.

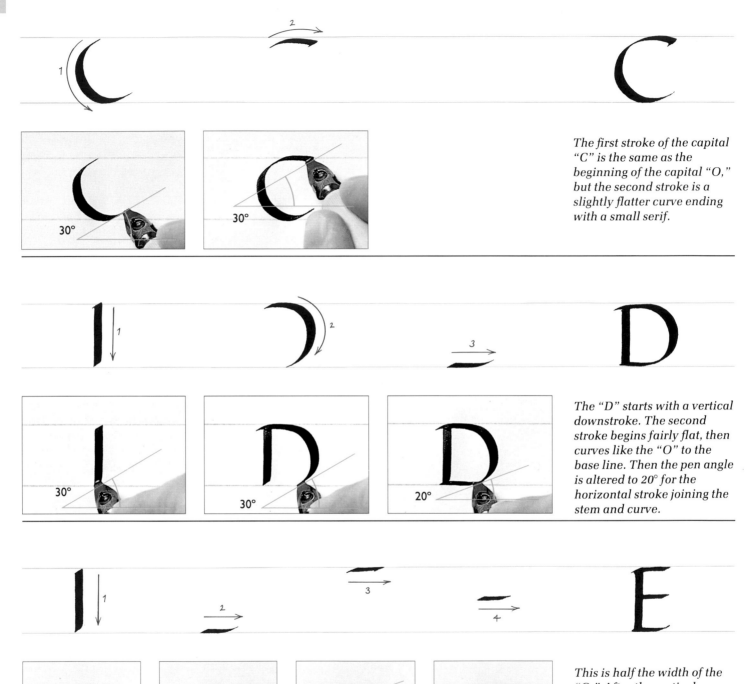

The first stroke of the capital "C" is the same as the beginning of the capital "O," but the second stroke is a slightly flatter curve ending with a small serif.

The "D" starts with a vertical downstroke. The second stroke begins fairly flat, then curves like the "O" to the base line. Then the pen angle is altered to 20° for the horizontal stroke joining the stem and curve.

This is half the width of the "O." After the vertical downstroke, change to 20° for the three horizontal strokes, with the bottom stroke slightly longer to balance the letter. The middle bar should be a little above halfway.

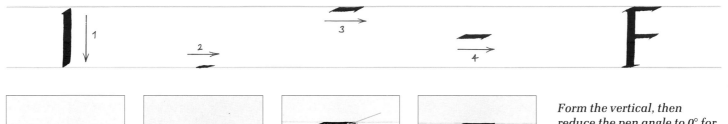

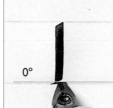 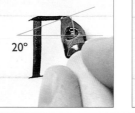

30° 0° 20° 20°

Form the vertical, then reduce the pen angle to 0° for a slab serif; fill in any gap with the edge of the nib. Form the two horizontal strokes with the pen at 20° to the base line. Add the middle bar slightly below halfway.

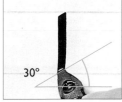 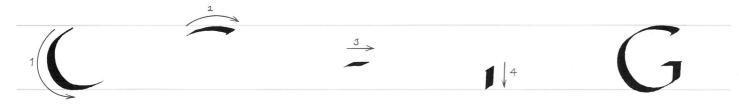

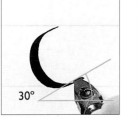 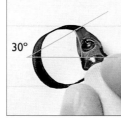 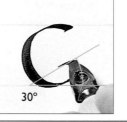 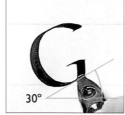

30° 30° 30° 30° 30°

For the capital "G," the first two strokes are the same as the letter "C," with a horizontal serif below halfway and a vertical downstroke joining the bottom tip of the first curve.

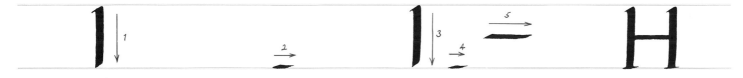

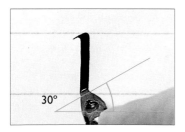 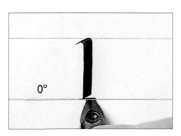 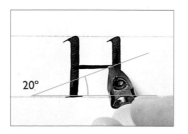

30° 0° 20°

A Roman capital "H" is three-quarters the size of the capital "O." Starting with hook serifs, the two vertical downstrokes end with 0° slab serifs. The crossbar should be slightly above halfway and at a 20° angle.

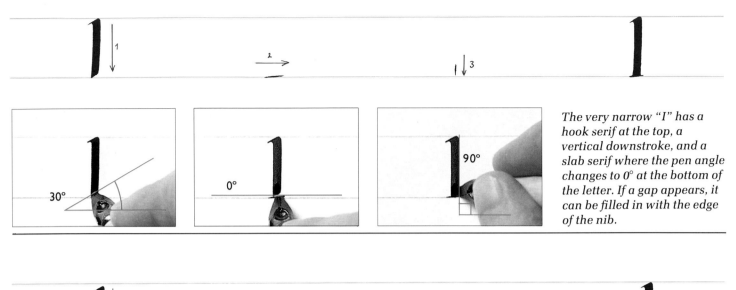

The very narrow "I" has a hook serif at the top, a vertical downstroke, and a slab serif where the pen angle changes to 0° at the bottom of the letter. If a gap appears, it can be filled in with the edge of the nib.

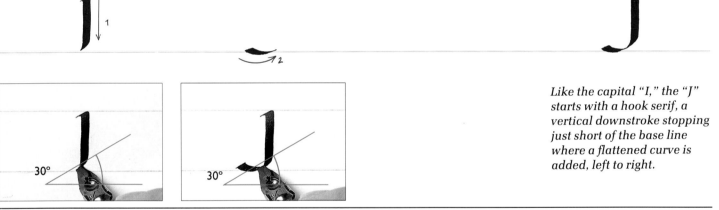

Like the capital "I," the "J" starts with a hook serif, a vertical downstroke stopping just short of the base line where a flattened curve is added, left to right.

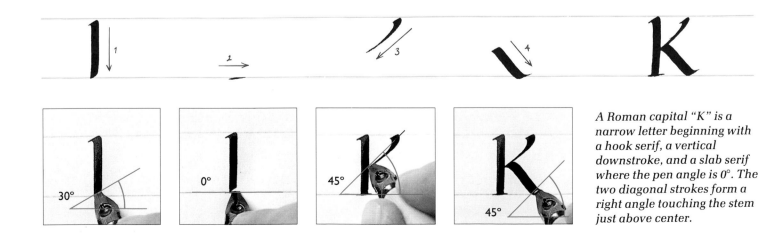

A Roman capital "K" is a narrow letter beginning with a hook serif, a vertical downstroke, and a slab serif where the pen angle is 0°. The two diagonal strokes form a right angle touching the stem just above center.

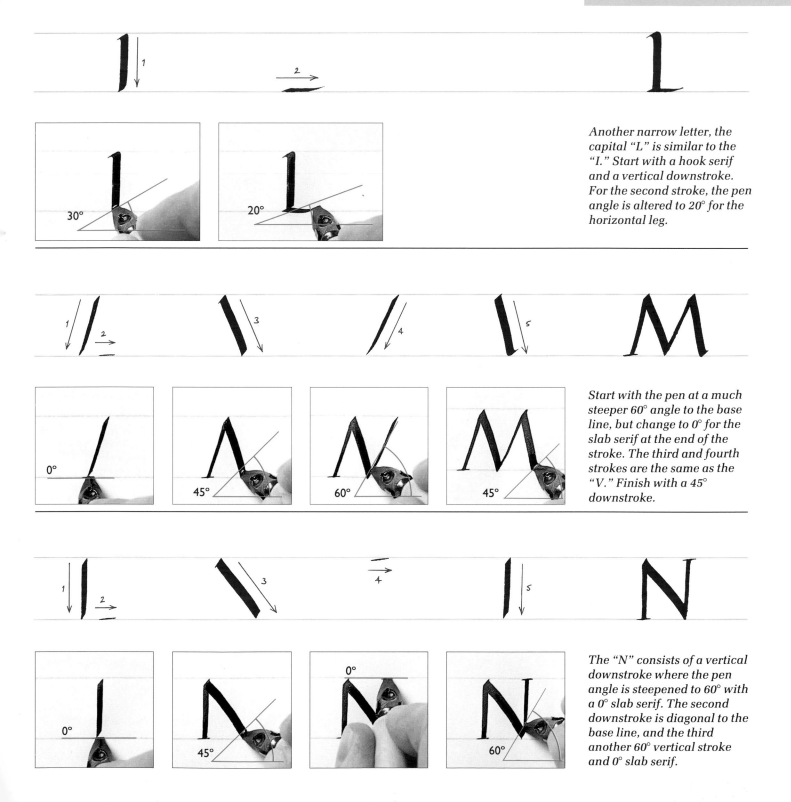

Another narrow letter, the capital "L" is similar to the "I." Start with a hook serif and a vertical downstroke. For the second stroke, the pen angle is altered to 20° for the horizontal leg.

Start with the pen at a much steeper 60° angle to the base line, but change to 0° for the slab serif at the end of the stroke. The third and fourth strokes are the same as the "V." Finish with a 45° downstroke.

The "N" consists of a vertical downstroke where the pen angle is steepened to 60° with a 0° slab serif. The second downstroke is diagonal to the base line, and the third another 60° vertical stroke and 0° slab serif.

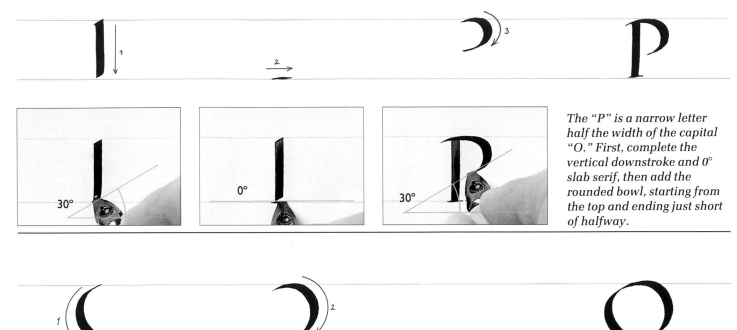

The "P" is a narrow letter half the width of the capital "O." First, complete the vertical downstroke and 0° slab serif, then add the rounded bowl, starting from the top and ending just short of halfway.

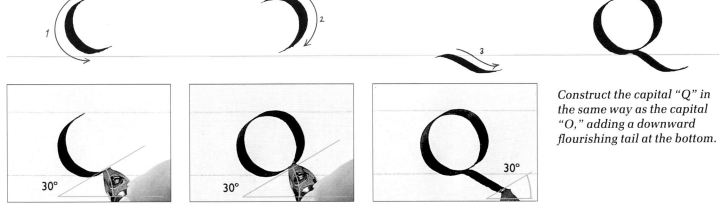

Construct the capital "Q" in the same way as the capital "O," adding a downward flourishing tail at the bottom.

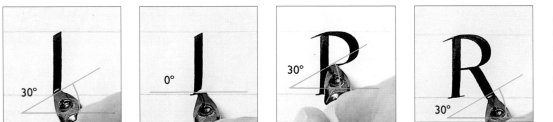

Here the vertical downstroke and the slab serif are the same as the "P," except the curve of the bowl meets the stem halfway down. Then add the tail springing from it to the base line.

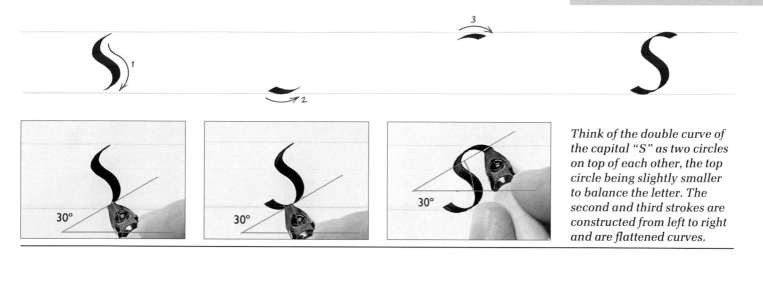

Think of the double curve of the capital "S" as two circles on top of each other, the top circle being slightly smaller to balance the letter. The second and third strokes are constructed from left to right and are flattened curves.

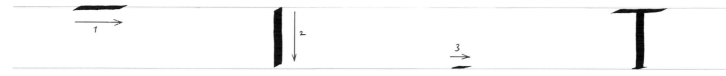

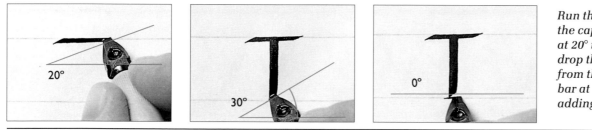

Run the crossbar just under the cap line with the pen held at 20° to the base line. Then drop the vertical downstroke from the center of the cross-bar at 30° to the base line, adding a final 0° slab serif.

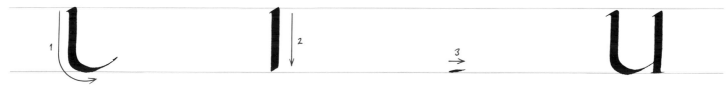

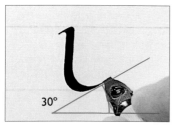
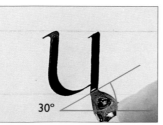
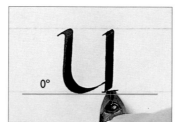

Start with a hook serif to the vertical downstroke curving like the "O" just before the base line. The second stroke is a hook serif, a vertical downstroke, and a 0° slab serif.

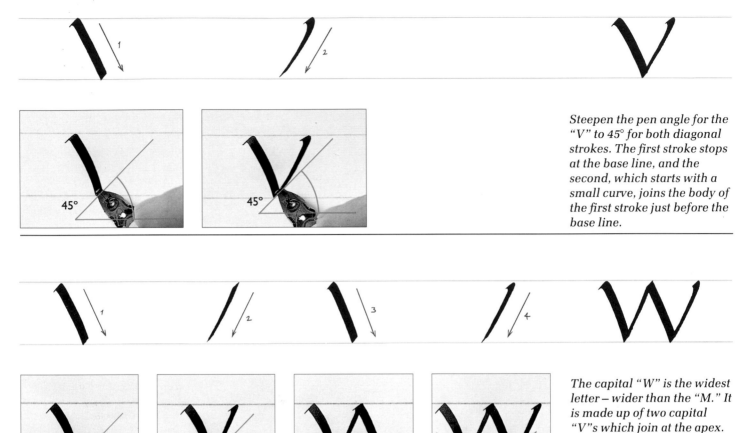

Steepen the pen angle for the "V" to 45° for both diagonal strokes. The first stroke stops at the base line, and the second, which starts with a small curve, joins the body of the first stroke just before the base line.

The capital "W" is the widest letter – wider than the "M." It is made up of two capital "V"s which join at the apex. Remember that the pen angle is steeper at 45°.

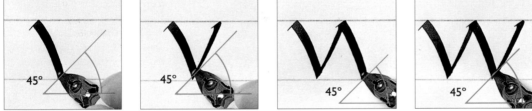

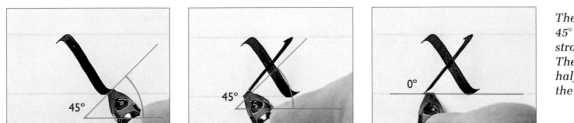

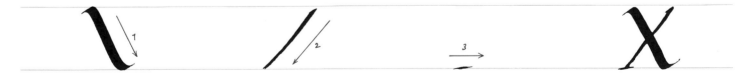

The pen is held at a steeper 45° angle for the diagonal strokes of the capital "X." The strokes cross just above halfway, which will balance the letter.

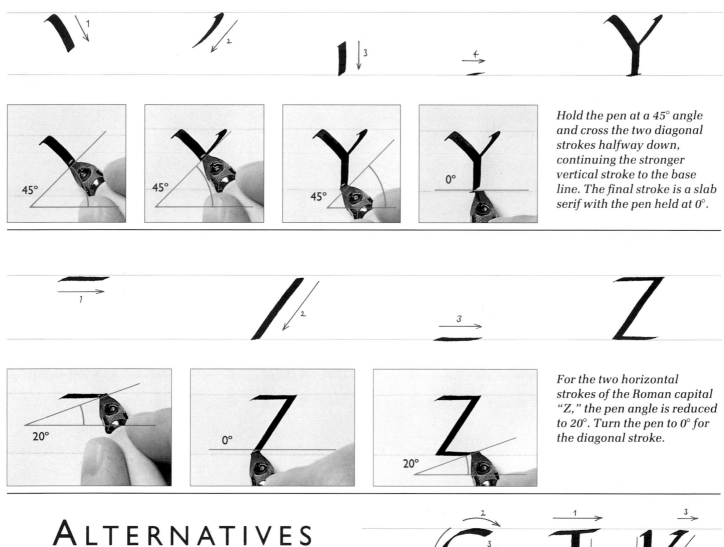

Hold the pen at a 45° angle and cross the two diagonal strokes halfway down, continuing the stronger vertical stroke to the base line. The final stroke is a slab serif with the pen held at 0°.

For the two horizontal strokes of the Roman capital "Z," the pen angle is reduced to 20°. Turn the pen to 0° for the diagonal stroke.

ALTERNATIVES

The Roman capital alphabet includes alternative letters with alternative serifs, such as the tops of the "V" and "W." Punctuation and numbers that match this alphabet are shown with the Versal alphabet (see page 165), constructed in the Roman style.

TROUBLESHOOTING

Most beginners have problems with the horizontal cross-bars of letters in the Roman capital alphabet, either making them too heavy or placing them in the wrong position. Another problem to watch for concerns the flat pen angle needed to form slab serifs. With a steeper pen angle, these serifs become too heavy. Remember to check that proportions are consistent between similar letters, such as diagonal letters like the "V" and "W."

The crossbar to this letter "H" has been constructed too high up so that the letter does not appear balanced.

H ×   H ×

Here the crossbar has been constructed too low down, making the letter look bottom-heavy.

CORRECT LETTERFORMS

ABCDEFGHIJKLM

B× C×

The top counter space of this letter "B" is far too large, which makes the letter appear top-heavy. The lower curve should be the larger one to balance the letter.

The top curve of the letter "C" is too steep and comes too far down, giving it a hooked appearance. It should be flatter and match that at the bottom.

G×

Here the small horizontal crossbar and vertical downstroke have been constructed far too high up the letter.

L×

The horizontal foot of the letter "L" has been written with the pen at far too steep an angle, which makes it look too heavy.

E×

The letter "E" has been constructed with the pen held at too steep an angle, making the arms too heavy.

This letter "U" has been constructed too narrow.

U ×

The second curve of this letter "O" is not rounded enough.

O ×

For the diagonal middle stroke of this letter "Z," the pen has been held at the wrong angle. It therefore looks far too thin.

Z ×

NOPQRSTUVWXYZ

The first stroke, the horizontal bar, of this letter "T" has been constructed with the pen held at too steep an angle (over 30°), making it look ugly and top-heavy.

T ×

The second stroke of the "V" has been added too near the first, making the letter too narrow.

V ×

Y ×

The two diagonal lines of this letter "Y" join too low down the letter, making it out of proportion.

GALLERY

Today's calligraphers have the advantage of over 2,000 years of the development of the Roman alphabet, and studying inscriptions can assist in a greater awareness of letterforms and designs. The examples shown here start with a traditional piece of Roman lettering for a memorial plaque, continuing to a dramatic and very modern interpretation of the style. It is appropriate to include a piece of carved lettering finishing with an elegant panel.

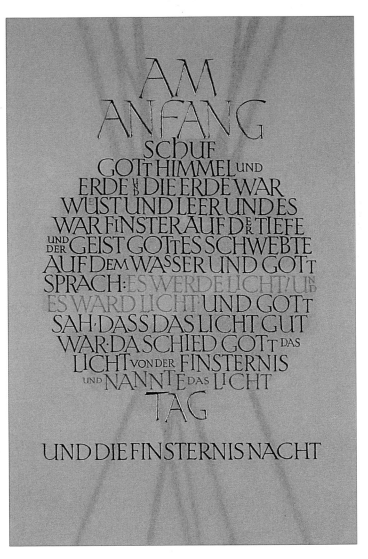

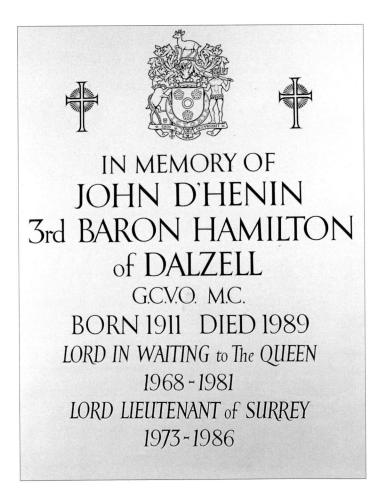

IN MEMORY OF
JOHN D'HENIN
3rd BARON HAMILTON
of DALZELL
G.C.V.O. M.C.
BORN 1911   DIED 1989
LORD IN WAITING to The QUEEN
1968 - 1981
LORD LIEUTENANT of SURREY
1973 - 1986

◀ **DESIGN FOR MEMORIAL IN BRASS**
Anthony Wood's traditional piece was commissioned, as the title suggests, for a memorial plaque. Produced in brass by an acid-etched engraving method, it is an excellent example of letterforms in various sizes, including compressed letters at the bottom. The coat of arms and the two crosses balance the work perfectly.

▲ **AM ANFANG**
This highly dramatic interpretation of "In the beginning" from Genesis was written in German by Mary White using a fine pen and brush with watercolors in a circular format. Small Roman letters make everything fit. The title and the bottom of the circle have been written in gesso and gold leaf, making the letters look beautifully raised.

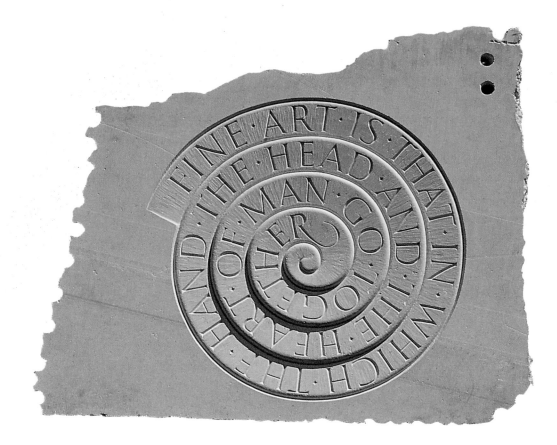

◀ QUOTATION
No section on Roman lettering would be complete without an example of a carved piece. This quotation from John Ruskin carved onto a found piece of Portland stone was very creatively designed in a spiral shape by Richard Kindersley. Diamond-shaped dots separate the words, which end with a superb flourish to the "R."

▼ QUOTATION
This elegant piece in Roman capitals has been designed in an asymmetrical layout for this quotation from Spectator by Joseph Addison. Erica Daulman used a round-hand steel nib on Saunders Waterford HP paper. These letters have very small slab serifs.

I VALUE MY GARDEN MORE FOR
BEING FULL OF BLACKBIRDS
    THAN OF CHERRIES, AND VERY
FRANKLY GIVE THEM FRUIT
    FOR THEIR SONGS   JOSEPH ADDISON

UNCIAL LETTERS

Alongside the graceful Roman capitals, another hand called Uncial thrived, descended from an ancient letterform. Uncial, from *uncia*, the Latin for "inch," was quick and easy to write, and its popularity coincided with the use of parchment as a writing surface. It was therefore used as the main book script between the 4th and 8th centuries A.D. The letters were capital forms using a flat or slightly angled pen. The Half Uncial majuscule was developed to increase the lettering speed of scribes. Rounded in style, it has more ascenders and descenders and acquired the appearance of lower-case letters.

MODERN UNCIAL

The main characteristics of the Modern Uncial style comprise a bold yet graceful rounded letterform using a flat pen angle. There are minimal ascenders and descenders, giving the appearance of an approachable yet formal script. Using a flat pen angle, this hand has a clean, sharp edge. It is written with a small x height and very simple hook serifs, making it quite legible.

ESSENTIAL INFORMATION

Round serif

O **B**

20° angle

Upright
0° slope

Letter height The x height is 3½ nib widths.
Basic pen angle The pen angle for most letters is 20°, with some horizontal strokes written at a slightly flatter 15° angle.
"O" form Here the "O" is slightly wider than a circle.
Slope This is an upright alphabet.
Serif forms Small round serifs are used here.
Letter groups The following letters are round and slightly wider than a circle: "O," "C," "D," and "E." The letters "G," "H," and "M" are even wider, and the group is completed by "N," "P," "Q," "T," "U," and "Y." The second group includes two-tier letters – "B," "R" and "S." The letters "A," "K," "V," "W," and "Z" are grouped together as diagonal letters, leaving "I," "F," "J," and "L" as the straight letters.

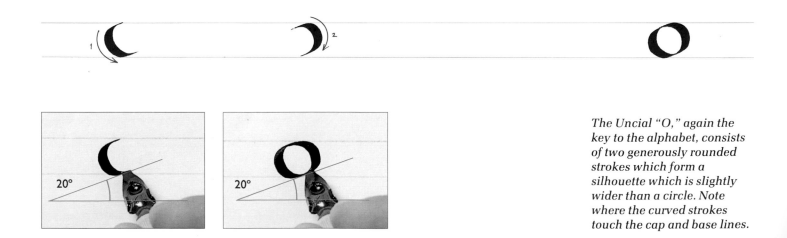

20°

20°

The Uncial "O," again the key to the alphabet, consists of two generously rounded strokes which form a silhouette which is slightly wider than a circle. Note where the curved strokes touch the cap and base lines.

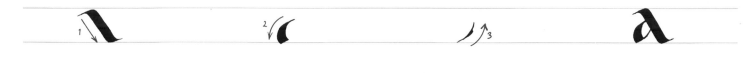

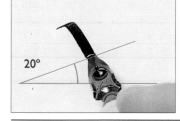 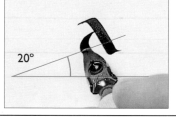 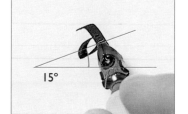

20° 20° 15°

Take a thin serif from the top of the cap line to the base line, finishing with another thin serif. Curve from just above halfway, down to the base line, then, with the edge of the pen, draw the ink up back into the main stem.

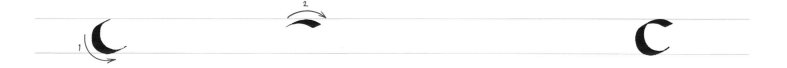

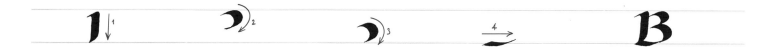

20° 20° 20° 15°

Start with a small round serif vertically to the base line. The curve forming the upper (smaller) bowl should join the stem slightly above halfway. The second curve is joined by a horizontal at a 15° angle from left to right.

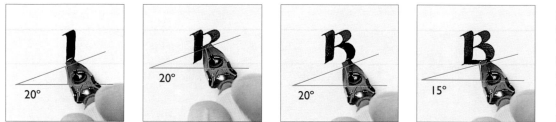

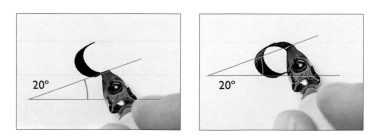

20° 20°

The main body of the "C" imitates the generous curve of the letter "O," but the second curve should be a little flatter.

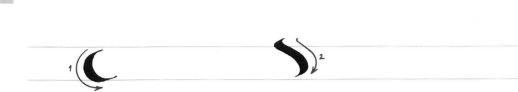

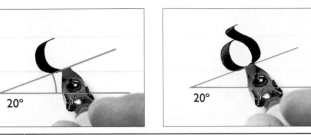

The first stroke of the "D" is the same as for "C." Start the second stroke approximately one nib width above the top of the cap line with a rounded serif, curving to join the first stroke.

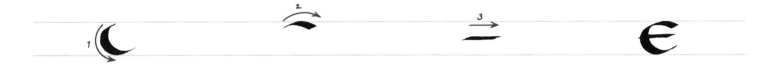

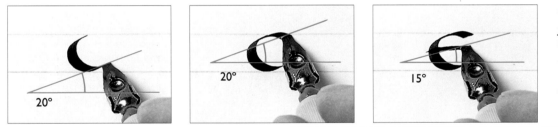

The letter "E" is made up from the first two strokes of the letter "C" with a horizontal crossbar added, with the pen held at 15°, slightly above halfway.

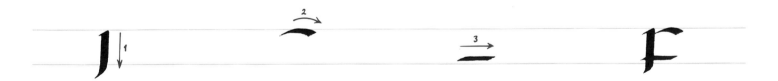

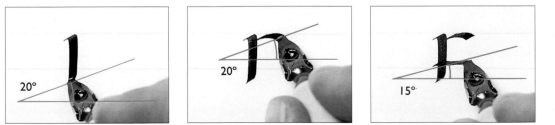

Start with a very small rounded serif ending just below the base line. The second stroke is similar to that of the "C." Add a horizontal crossbar, with the pen held at 15°, to the stem just above the base line.

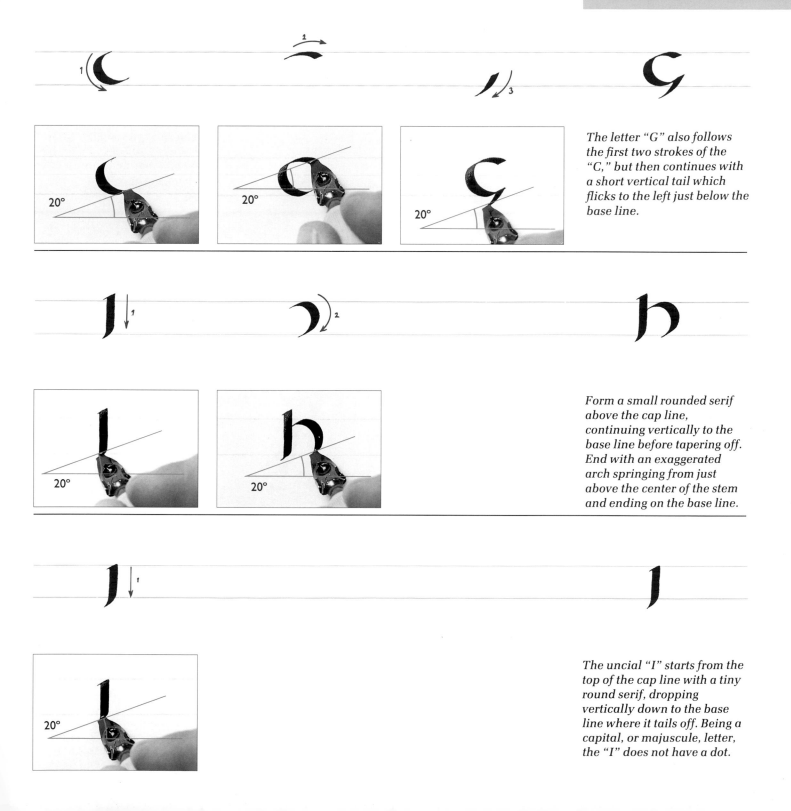

The letter "G" also follows the first two strokes of the "C," but then continues with a short vertical tail which flicks to the left just below the base line.

Form a small rounded serif above the cap line, continuing vertically to the base line before tapering off. End with an exaggerated arch springing from just above the center of the stem and ending on the base line.

The uncial "I" starts from the top of the cap line with a tiny round serif, dropping vertically down to the base line where it tails off. Being a capital, or majuscule, letter, the "I" does not have a dot.

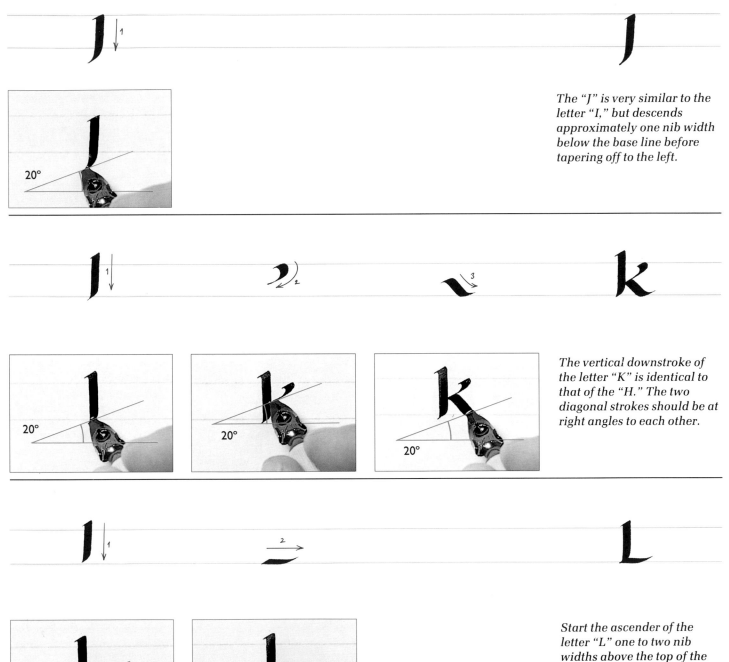

The "J" is very similar to the letter "I," but descends approximately one nib width below the base line before tapering off to the left.

The vertical downstroke of the letter "K" is identical to that of the "H." The two diagonal strokes should be at right angles to each other.

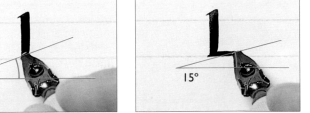

Start the ascender of the letter "L" one to two nib widths above the top of the cap line with a tiny round serif, then drop the vertical downstroke to the base line. Then turn the pen slightly to 15° for the horizontal bar.

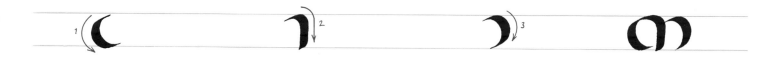

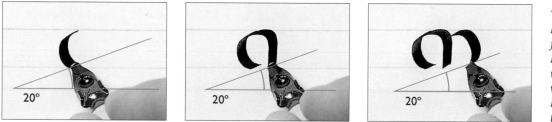

This is one of the widest letters of the alphabet. The first stroke curves like the letter "O." The second starts with a curve, changing to the vertical to end on the base line. The third curve imitates the rounded stroke of the "H."

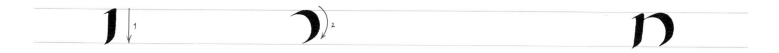

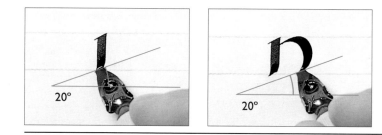

The "N" begins with the first stroke of the letter "I," followed by the second rounded curve of the letter "H."

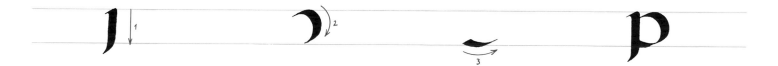

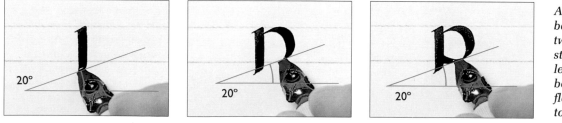

A tiny round serif descends below the base line by one to two nib widths. The second stroke is the same as the letters "H" and "N." The bowl is completed by a flattened curve from the stem to the point of the curve.

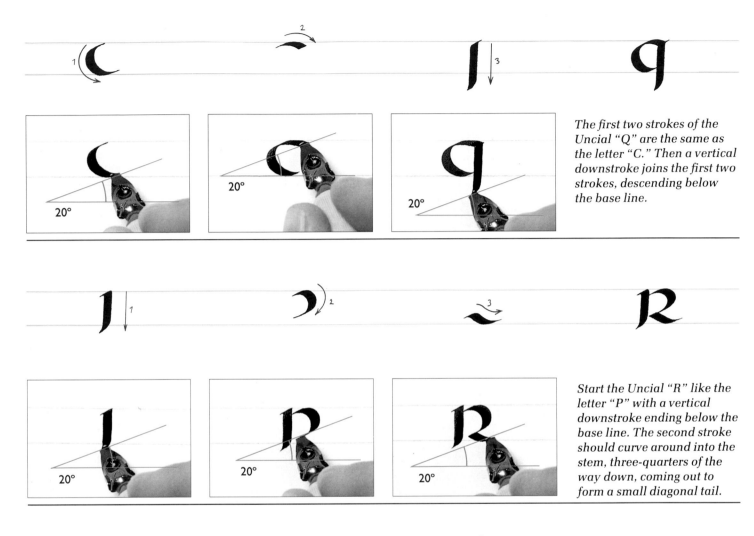

The first two strokes of the Uncial "Q" are the same as the letter "C." Then a vertical downstroke joins the first two strokes, descending below the base line.

Start the Uncial "R" like the letter "P" with a vertical downstroke ending below the base line. The second stroke should curve around into the stem, three-quarters of the way down, coming out to form a small diagonal tail.

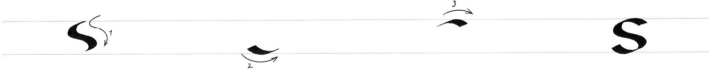

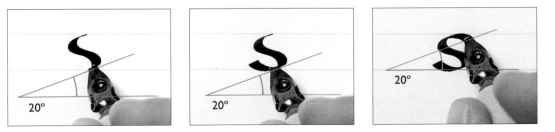

Start below the cap line, curving right and then left to end above the base line. Add flattened curves joining the letter from left to right, just breaking through the base line to make the bottom counter larger.

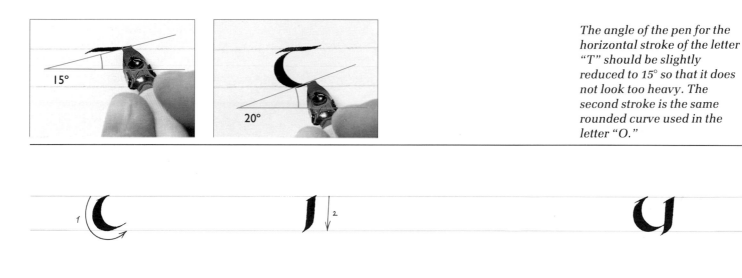

The angle of the pen for the horizontal stroke of the letter "T" should be slightly reduced to 15° so that it does not look too heavy. The second stroke is the same rounded curve used in the letter "O."

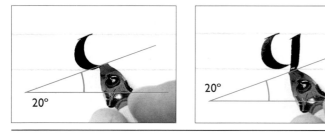

The letter "U" begins with a thin serif, then curves around like the letter "C." The second stroke is identical to the letter "I," connecting to the curve at the point.

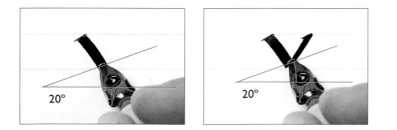

The Uncial "V" consists of two diagonal strokes, the second stroke joining the first just before the base line. Keep this letter quite wide to match the width of the other letters.

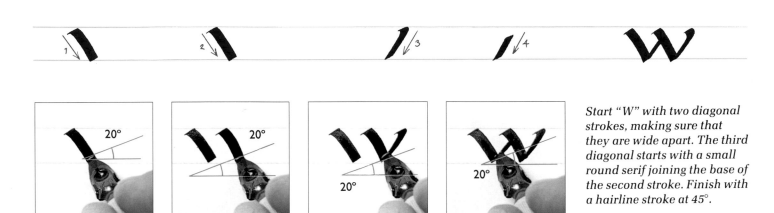

Start "W" with two diagonal strokes, making sure that they are wide apart. The third diagonal starts with a small round serif joining the base of the second stroke. Finish with a hairline stroke at 45°.

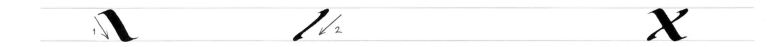

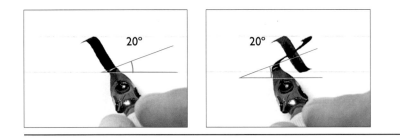

The two diagonal strokes of the Uncial "X" cross just above halfway. The second diagonal begins and ends with a small round serif.

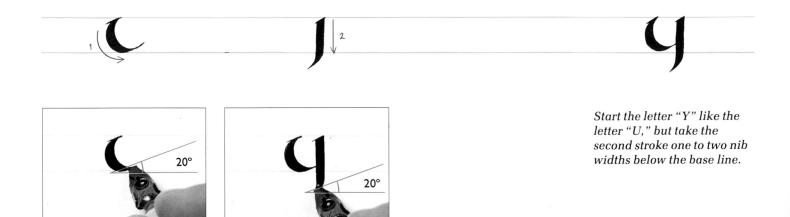

Start the letter "Y" like the letter "U," but take the second stroke one to two nib widths below the base line.

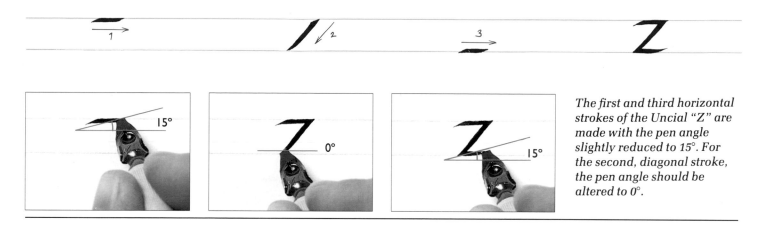

The first and third horizontal strokes of the Uncial "Z" are made with the pen angle slightly reduced to 15°. For the second, diagonal stroke, the pen angle should be altered to 0°.

ALTERNATIVES

Alternative Modern Uncial letterforms should be kept simple and in character with the rest of the alphabet. Care must be taken to write both numbers and punctuation marks using the flatter pen angle of this alphabet.

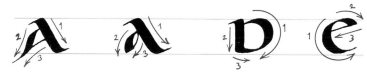

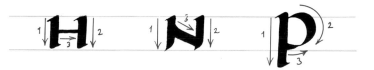

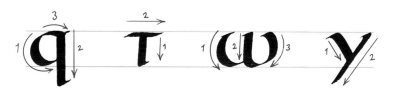

AMPERSANDS

PUNCTUATION

NUMERALS

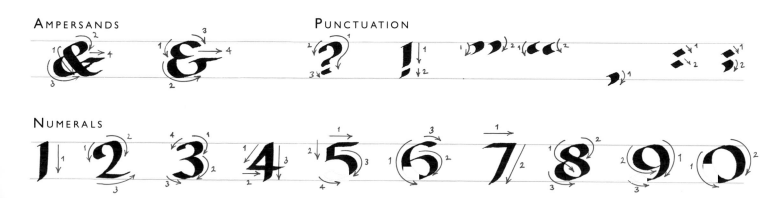

TROUBLESHOOTING

This is a very flat-angled, rounded alphabet, so special attention should be given to the rounded bowls of letters such as "B" and "R." There is a tendency when learning to construct this alphabet too narrow; it needs to be as generously rounded and balanced as you can make it. The simple hook serifs for this alphabet are small, and it is most important that they are not over-emphasized.

The horizontal crossbar to the letter "F" has been constructed too high up the stem. It should have been added just above the base line.

F

CORRECT LETTERFORMS

abcdefghijklm

The top bowl of this letter "B" is too big, making the whole letter look top-heavy.

B

The second stroke of the letter "D" should be more rounded, similar to the first. This makes the letter look too narrow.

d

To maintain the characteristic roundness of this script, the second stroke of the letter "H" needs to be more generously curved, going out before coming in.

h

The horizontal bar of the letter "E" has been written too high up the curve of the letter, making it look as if it is closing up.

The bowl of the letter "R" here is far too small. It should curve around generously to just above the base line, giving the letter the rounded look which is characteristic of this alphabet.

R ×

For the diagonal middle stroke of this letter "Z," the pen has been held at too steep an angle; this makes it look far too thin.

Z ×

n o p q r s t u v w x y z

The first curve of this letter "Q" is not round enough, making the vertical downstroke too close and the counter area too small.

The two diagonal strokes of this "W" have been constructed too close together; therefore, the letter does not balance.

The vertical downstroke has been added too near the first curve, which makes the letter look too narrow.

HALF UNCIAL

This hand is closely linked to the Celtic Insular style which achieved a high level of excellence as practiced by the Irish and Northumbria scribes from the 6th to the 8th centuries A.D. It can be seen in its most developed form in such superb examples as the Book of Kells, the Lindisfarne Gospels, and the Book of Durrow.

The flatter 5° pen angle of the Half Uncial will enable the student to achieve these simply constructed letterforms which are very rounded in character – beautiful shapes which look so graceful. This hand is very free-flowing, starting with wedge-shaped serifs and slightly longer ascenders and descenders than the Modern Uncial, which allows it to be written with greater ease.

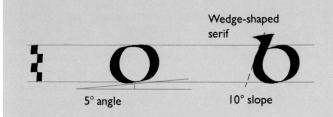

ESSENTIAL INFORMATION

Wedge-shaped serif

5° angle   10° slope

Letter height The x height is 4 nib widths.
Basic pen angle The pen angle for this alphabet is 5°.
"O" form The letter "O" is slightly wider than a circle.
Slope Most letters are written upright with the exception of the letters "B" and "L," which have a forward slant.
Serif forms Wedge-shaped serifs are added to these letters.
Letter groups The round letters here are as follows: "O," "A," "C," "D," "E," "G," "H," "P," "Q," "T," "U," "W," and "Y." The two-tier letters are "S" and "R" and the straight letters "F," "I," "J," "M," and "N." The letters "B" and "L" have a left slant and the diagonal letter group includes "K," "V," "X," and "Z."

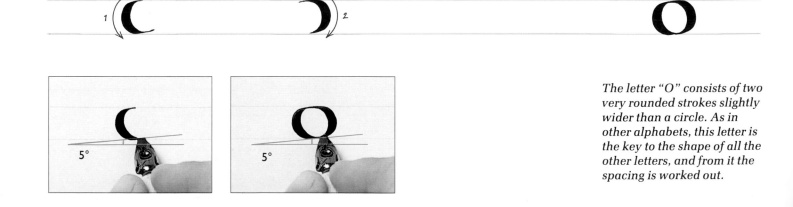

The letter "O" consists of two very rounded strokes slightly wider than a circle. As in other alphabets, this letter is the key to the shape of all the other letters, and from it the spacing is worked out.

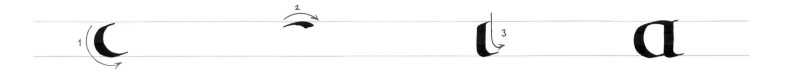

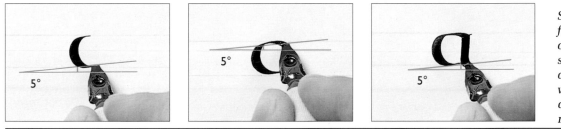

Start with a rounded curve for the bowl with a flatter curve at the top. The third stroke starts with a thin serif at the top of the x line, drops vertically to the base line, and finishes with a small rounded serif.

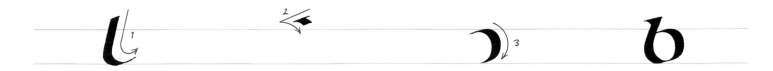

The ascender of "B" has a 10° slant toward the base line, curving to the right just before it. Add a wedge-shaped serif. The final stroke is the right-hand curve of the "O," joining the bowl to the main body of the letter.

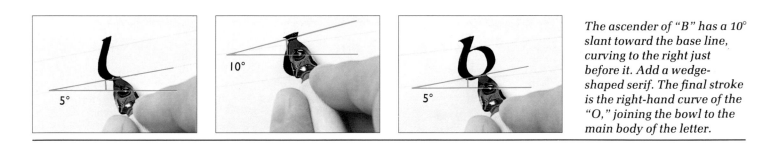

The letter "C" starts the same as the letter "O" with a generous curve ending in a point. The letter is completed with a flattened curve, balancing the bottom stroke.

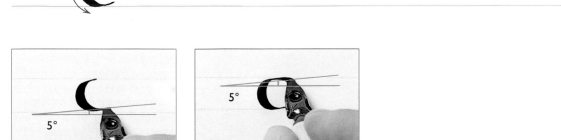

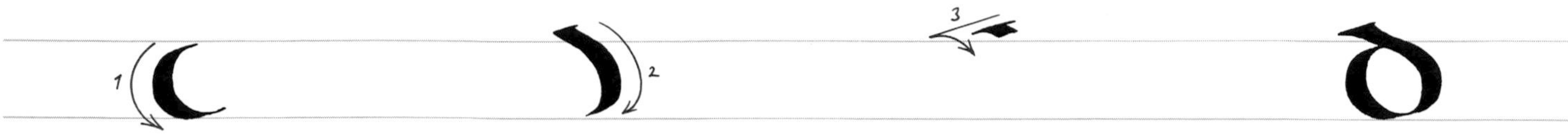

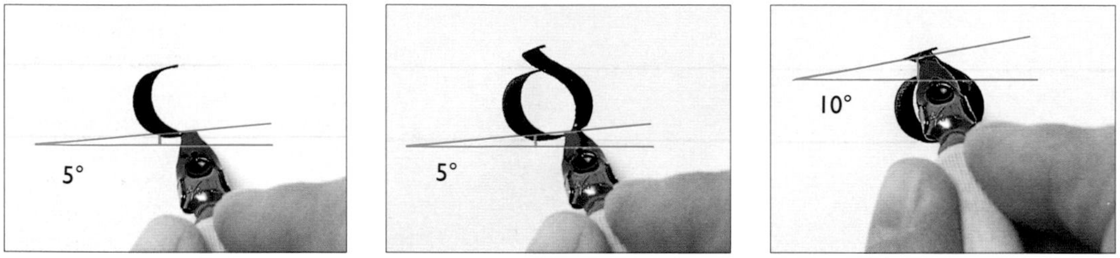

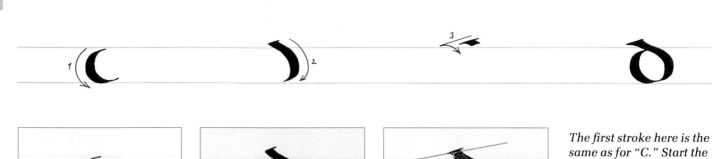

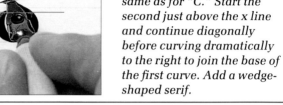

The first stroke here is the same as for "C." Start the second just above the x line and continue diagonally before curving dramatically to the right to join the base of the first curve. Add a wedge-shaped serif.

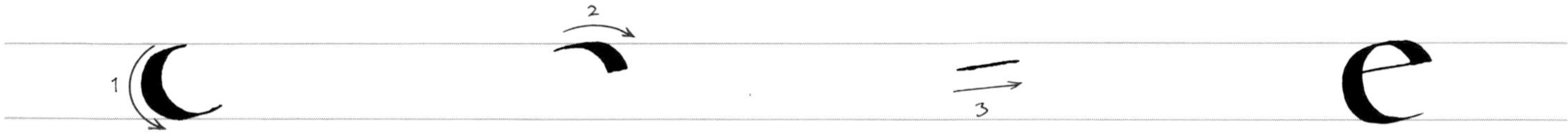

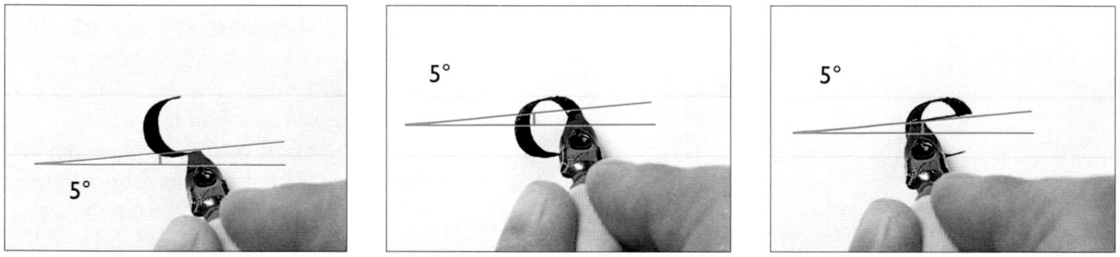

This "E" starts off the same as the letters "O" and "C." The second stroke is approximately a quarter of the right-hand curve of the "O." A horizontal hairline completes the letter.

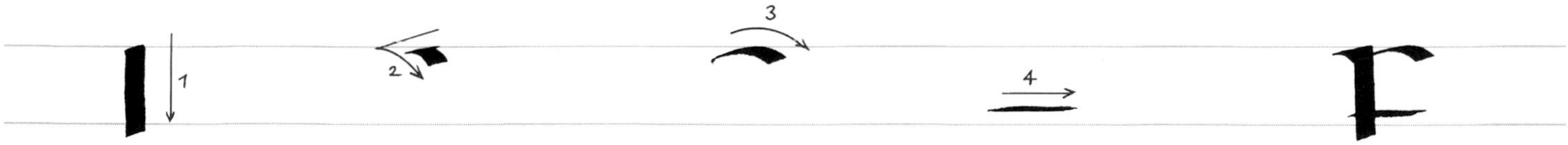

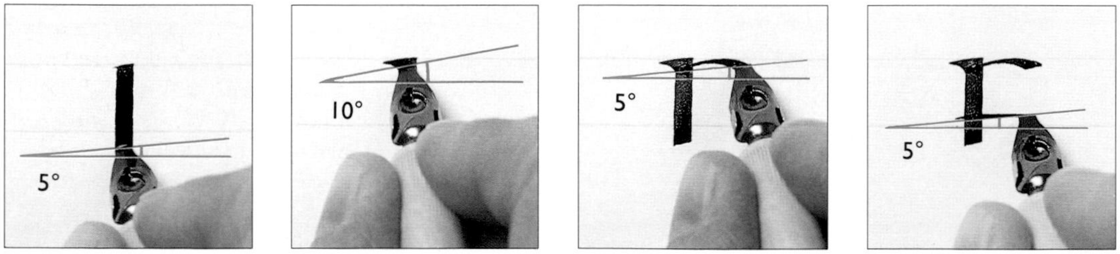

Take a vertical to just below the base line to form a very short descender; add a wedge-shaped serif. Curve out gently from just below the top of the stem and end with a crossbar at 5° to the horizontal.

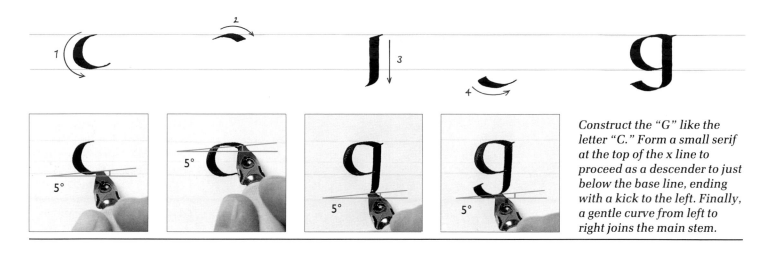

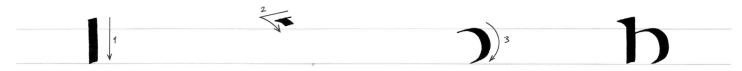

Construct the "G" like the letter "C." Form a small serif at the top of the x line to proceed as a descender to just below the base line, ending with a kick to the left. Finally, a gentle curve from left to right joins the main stem.

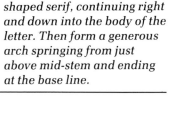

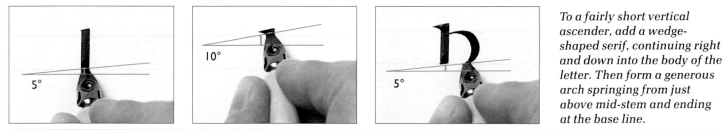

To a fairly short vertical ascender, add a wedge-shaped serif, continuing right and down into the body of the letter. Then form a generous arch springing from just above mid-stem and ending at the base line.

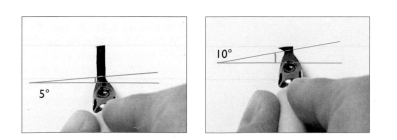

The main stem of the letter "I" comes down in a single stroke from the top of the x line to the base line. The next stroke is the wedge-shaped serif, a thin line continuing right and down into the stem of the letter.

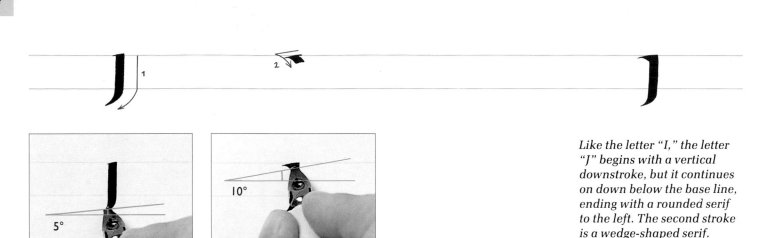

Like the letter "I," the letter "J" begins with a vertical downstroke, but it continues on down below the base line, ending with a rounded serif to the left. The second stroke is a wedge-shaped serif.

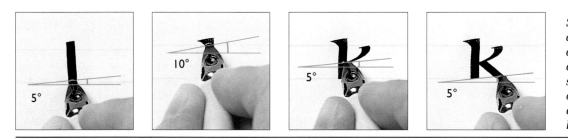

Start with a short vertical ascender; add a wedge serif at the top. A third of the way down and to the right of the stem, curve around to meet it on the diagonal. Continue diagonally to just brush the base line.

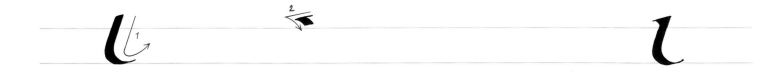

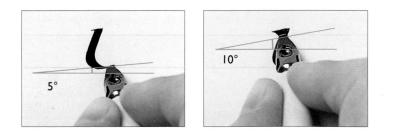

The Half Uncial "L," like the "B," begins with an ascender which slants approximately 10° from the vertical down toward the base line, curving to the right and then tapering to a point. A wedge-shaped serif is then added.

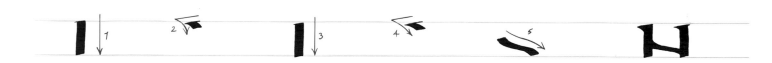

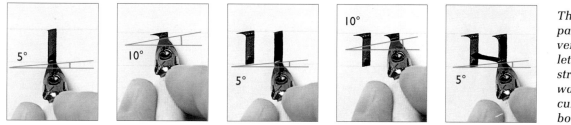

The first two strokes of the letter "M" are the same as the letter "I." The third and fourth strokes spring from just below the top of the stem to arch and then drop vertically down to the base line.

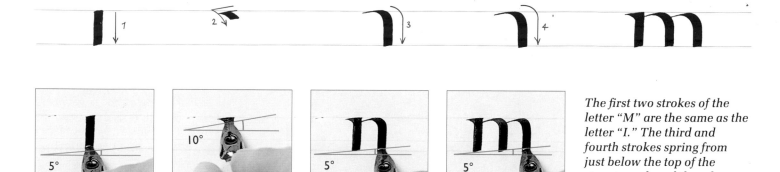

The letter "N" consists of two parallel letter "I" strokes vertically positioned the letter "O" apart. The final stroke starts just below half-way down the first vertical, curving diagonally to the bottom of the second vertical.

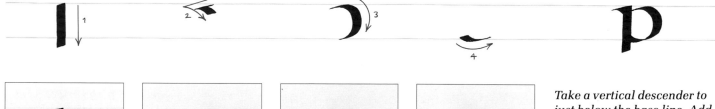

Take a vertical descender to just below the base line. Add a wedge serif and the bowl, from just below the top of the stem curving around to the base line. Starting from the stem, continue to the right to join the hairline of the curve.

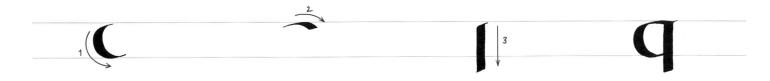

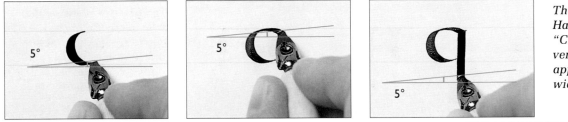

The first two strokes of the Half Uncial "Q" form a letter "C." The last stroke forms a vertical descender, ending approximately one to two nib widths below the base line.

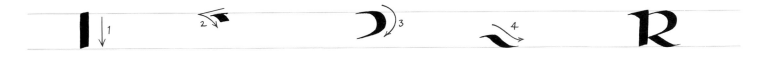

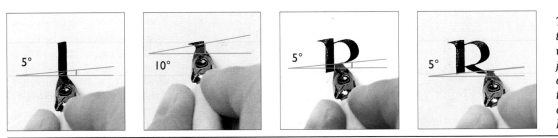

Take a vertical downstroke to the base line, and add a wedge-shaped serif. From just below the top, curve around to the stem just above the base line. End with a diagonal stroke tapering to a hairline point.

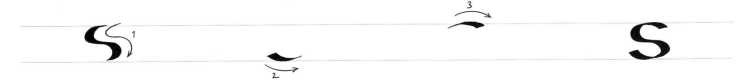

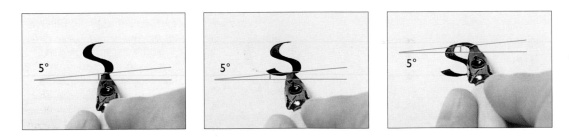

The body of the letter "S" begins with a left-hand curve, flattened in the middle, then curving again to end just above the base line. The top and bottom curves are slightly flattened and connect at the hairlines.

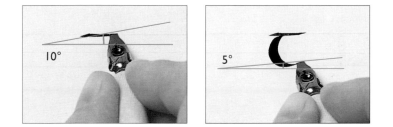

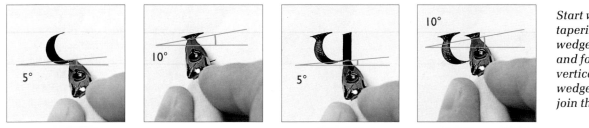

The letter "T" starts with a thin line serif and then continues with a horizontal stroke through the top of the x line. The letter is completed with a rounded curve the same as the letter "C."

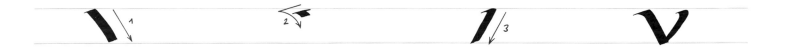

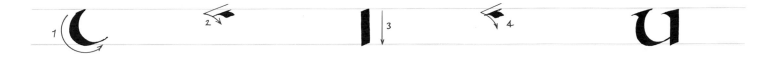

Start with a generous curve tapering to a hairline; add a wedge-shaped serif. The third and fourth strokes comprise a vertical downstroke and a wedge-shaped serif which join the curve at the hairline.

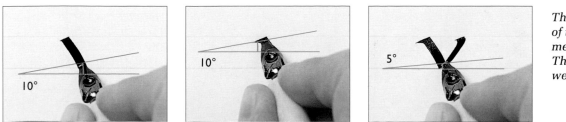

The Half Uncial "V" consists of two diagonal strokes which meet just above the base line. The first diagonal has a wedge-shaped serif added.

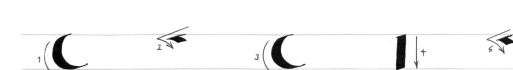

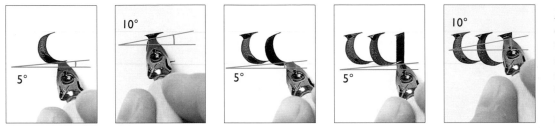

Begin like the letter "U," adding an extra curved stroke with a wedge-shaped serif before the vertical downstroke to the base line. Complete the letter with a wedge serif joining the curve at the hairline.

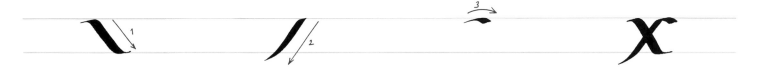

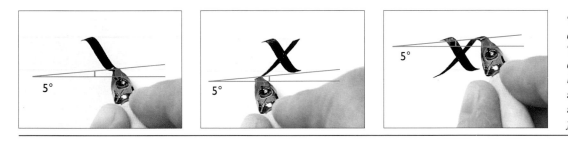

This consists of two diagonals crossing just above halfway. The second, thinner stroke descends to just below the base line. Take the third stroke from the top of the second, forming a small flattened curve.

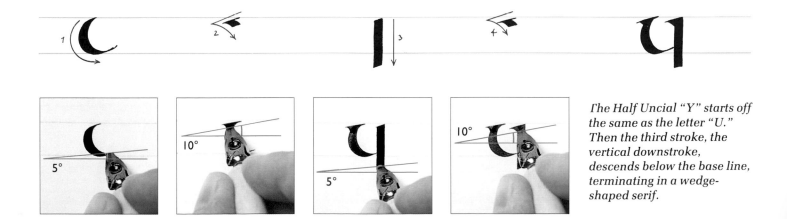

The Half Uncial "Y" starts off the same as the letter "U." Then the third stroke, the vertical downstroke, descends below the base line, terminating in a wedge-shaped serif.

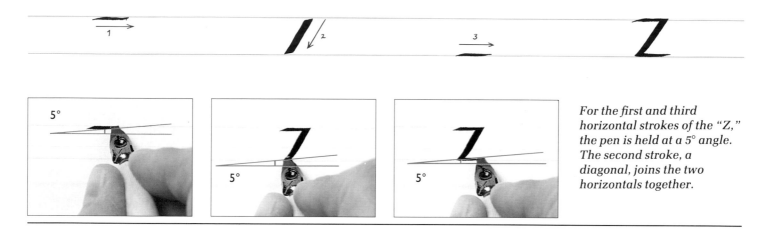

For the first and third horizontal strokes of the "Z," the pen is held at a 5° angle. The second stroke, a diagonal, joins the two horizontals together.

ALTERNATIVES

Half Uncial alternative letters need to be kept legible, with wedge-shaped serifs to match the rest of the alphabet. The punctuation marks and numbers need to be written within the writing height with the same flat, wide characteristic shape of the rest of the alphabet.

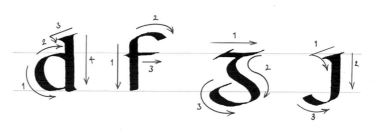

AMPERSANDS   PUNCTUATION

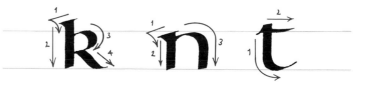

NUMERALS

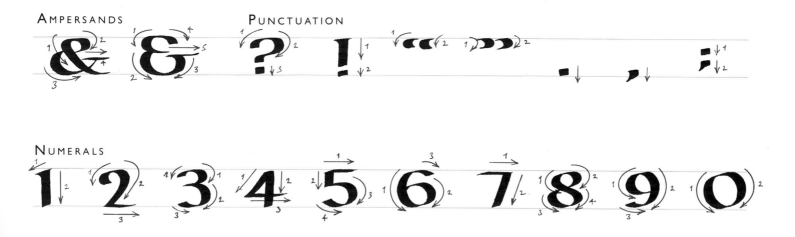

TROUBLESHOOTING

Like the Uncial alphabet, the Half Uncial is written with a very flat pen angle, and it takes some practice to get the balance of the letter shapes correct. Take care to balance the top strokes of the letters "C" and "E" with the bottom curve, as they have a tendency to be hooked, with the bowls of these letters too spread out. With the "R" and "K," the opposite problem occurs; the bowls of these letters are often too constricted. The wedge-shaped serifs are difficult to keep even and need plenty of practice.

The top diagonal stroke of the letter "K" is too small, making the second diagonal appear much too long.

CORRECT LETTERFORMS

abcdefghijklm

The top curve of the letter "C" is too hooked down, making the letter appear to fall over.

The horizontal crossbar of the letter "F" has been constructed too high up the stem.

The letter "M" needs to be balanced on both sides.

The counter space of the letter "E" is too large, giving the letter an unbalanced look.

The left-hand curve of the letter "T" needs to be generous, which will make the stroke longer.

The two vertical downstrokes of the letter "N" have been spaced too far apart, which makes the letter look too wide.

The two vertical downstrokes of this letter "N" have been spaced too close together. The letter is now too narrow.

The vertical downstroke of this "Y" has been constructed too close to the first curve, making the inside bowl too small.

NOPQRSTUVWXYZ

The bowl of the letter "R" is too small and the diagonal leg far too long, making the letter look unbalanced.

The letter "Z" has been constructed at the wrong angle, making the horizontal strokes too heavy and the diagonal too thin.

The horizontal strokes of this letter are the right distance apart but far too long, so they do not form a balanced letter.

GALLERY

Represented in this gallery section are various works using Uncial styles of writing, starting with a Half Uncial traditional work with its characteristic wedge-shaped serifs, and including large Celtic capitals which have been greatly influenced by the Book of Kells and the Lindis-farne Gospels. An interesting way of representing the alphabets is combining subtle backgrounds and incor-porating other styles as a contrast to the effect of the text.

▼ THIS NIGHT IS
This work by Paul Shaw is an example of extremely well-written Half Uncials and Celtic capitals. Although very traditional in layout and design, it was particularly appropriate for his client, as it was commissioned for reproduction in "Feasts and Seasons" magazine in 1984. Metal nibs were used with India ink on plate Bristol board. The author also used technical pens, and the illustrations are modeled on those in the Book of Kells.

▶ I HAVE A HUT
Doreen Howley's background treatment of the text makes a more interesting interpretation of this particular poem. A variety of different sizes of writing has been used with gouache written on top of a soft pastel background on watercolor paper.

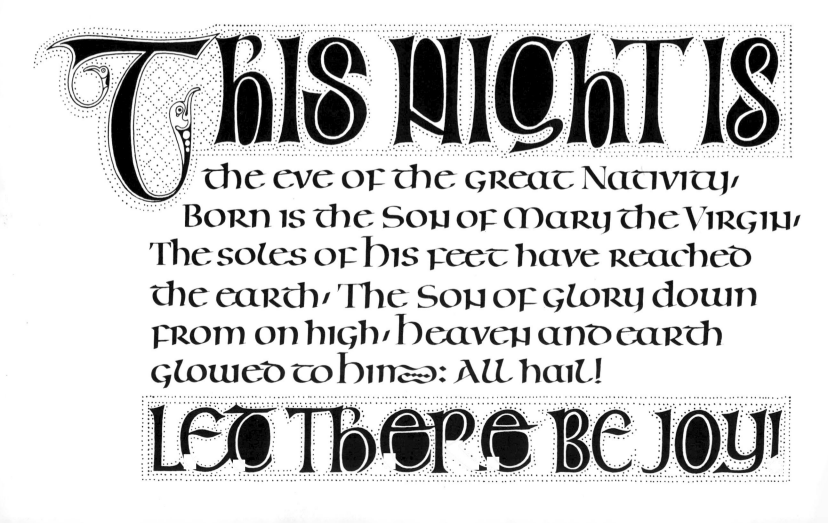

This night is the eve of the great Nativity, Born is the Son of Mary the Virgin, The soles of his feet have reached the earth, The Son of glory down from on high, Heaven and earth glowed to him: All hail! LET THERE BE JOY!

I HAVE A HUT
IN THE WOOD.
NONE·KNOWS·IT·BUT·MY·LORD:
AN ASH TREE THIS SIDE, A HAZEL ON THE OTHER,
A GREAT TREE ON A MOUND ENCLOSES IT,
TWO HEATHERY DOOR POSTS FOR SUPPORT,
AND A LINTEL OF HONEYSUCKLE:
· AROUND ITS CLOSE ·
THE WOOD SHEDS ITS NUTS
UPON FAT SWINE
THE SIZE OF MY HUT, SMALL YET NOT SMALL:
A PLACE OF FAMILIAR PATHS.
THE SHE BIRD IN ITS DRESS OF BLACKBIRD COLOUR
SINGS A MELODIOUS STRAIN FROM ITS GABLE.

FROM IRISH 10th CENTURY

SONG OF THE SOUL,
the Dark night of the soul

how well know that spring that
runs and overflows:
although its night, although its night, although its night,
spring that's eternal, hidden, and yet
how well i know from where it flows,
although its night, although its night, although its night,
i do not know its source: it has none;
everything else springs from it,
although its night, although its night, although its night,
i know that nothing else can be so lovely,
and that the earth and heavens drink its beauty,
although its night, although its night, although its night,
how well i know its deep and bottomless,
so deep no one can cross it,
although its night, although its night, although its night,
so clear it is, and never shadowed;
all light, i know, comes from it,
although its night, although its night, although its night,
so rich are its brimming waters that it gives
life to hell and heaven and every people,
although its night, although its night, although its night,
and the stream whose source was in this spring,
i know how powerful it is,
although its night, although its night, although its night,
and from these two a third stream rises,
but the first two are not greater,
although its night, although its night, although its night,
and that eternal spring is hidden
within this living bread to give us life,
although its night, although its night, although its night,
here it is crying out to every creature
to drink these waters because its dark,
although its night, although its night, although its night,
the living waters of the spring that i desire
i clearly see within this bread of life,
although its night, although its night, although its night,

SAN JAUN DE LA CRUZ

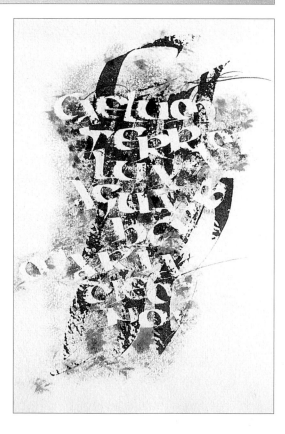

◄ GENESIS
This Latin quotation from
Genesis has been written by
Jonathan Bulfin in an
Uncial style initially using
masking fluid on watercolor
paper. Watercolor inks have
then been applied on top of
the lettering in various colors.
When the inks are dry, the
masking fluid is removed,
revealing the white paper
below.

▲ SONG OF THE SOUL
Mike Kecseg's personalized
versions of an Uncial style
written in white gouache
combined with a Gothic style
in black positioned between
the lines give a perfect
arrangement to the text by
San Juan de la Cruz. The
Gothic letters reflect the
dramatic verse with a
deliberate and well-executed
up and down movement.

GOTHIC SCRIPT

This alphabet is sometimes called "Blackletter" or "Old English." The Gothic hand developed slowly between the 12th and 15th centuries reflecting the pointed arches of Gothic architecture. It evolved from the more rounded Carolingian hand, becoming, by the 13th century, more condensed and, by the 14th century, more angular with square feet and heads. The condensed nature of this alphabet allowed more words to the page, therefore fewer pages and cheaper books. There are many variations of the Gothic script, such as cursive, which has more of a pointed shape, and Rotunda, which is more rounded.

In modern-day use, Gothic lettering has its limitations, although it can be particularly suited to festive occasions when decorative lettering is required.

LOWERCASE

The Gothic lower case is a very strong and angular alphabet made up of straight vertical lines where the pen is held at a constant 40° angle, together with small diagonal or diamond feet and shoulders. These repetitive strokes allow the calligrapher to develop a rhythm when writing and, with the letters being spaced close together, it gives a textured or patterned appearance. The disadvantage of this script is that with short ascenders and descenders and because it is compressed, it is sometimes considered hard to read. However, Gothic lower case does have the advantage of being probably the easiest script to learn.

In addition, because of the consistent vertical lines, it is a good style to improve both letter and word spacing, as it has equal areas of white space (counters) both inside and between the letters.

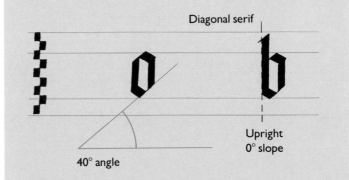

ESSENTIAL INFORMATION

Diagonal serif

Upright
0° slope

40° angle

Letter height The x height here is 5 nib widths; the ascenders and descenders are an extra 2 to 2½ nib widths.
Basic pen angle The pen angle between the nib and the writing line is 40°, and 30° for crossbars.
"O" form The letter "o" has a shape approximating a parallelogram.
Slope This is an upright alphabet where the letters are constructed vertical to the writing line.
Serif forms Small line serifs and small diagonal serifs are a feature of this alphabet.
Letter groups The Gothic lower-case alphabet is unusual, in that all the letters relate to the "o" form.

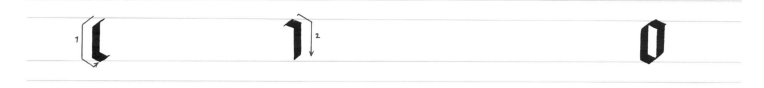

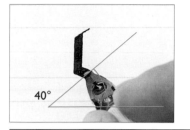

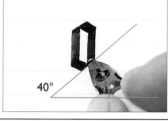

The counter of the basic Gothic lower-case "o" is a parallelogram, a four-sided figure with opposite sides parallel and equal. This distinctive, angular letter consists of two strokes, a vertical altering course to a diagonal ending on the base line. The second stroke this time starts diagonally and proceeds vertically to meet up with the first stroke.

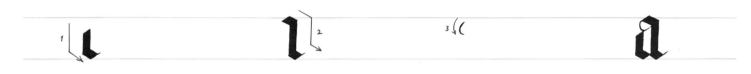

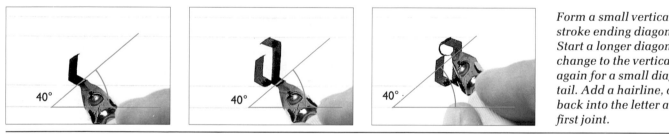

Form a small vertical down-stroke ending diagonally. Start a longer diagonal, change to the vertical, and again for a small diagonal tail. Add a hairline, arched back into the letter at the first joint.

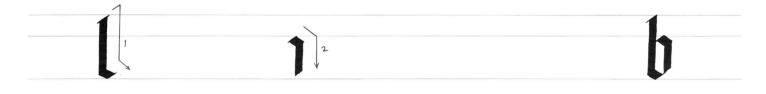

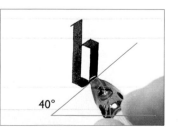

The letter "b" starts with a line serif on the ascender line dropping vertically to one nib width above the base line, where the stroke changes to the diagonal. Take the second stroke from the stem with the top edge of the nib on the x line, and make a diagonal to mirror that on the opposite side of the bowl. Drop down vertically, thus joining the two strokes.

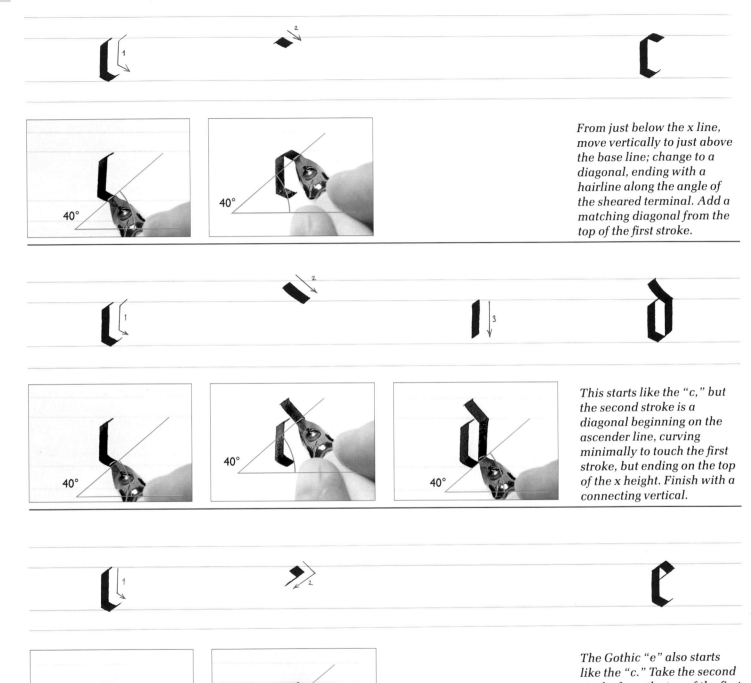

From just below the x line, move vertically to just above the base line; change to a diagonal, ending with a hairline along the angle of the sheared terminal. Add a matching diagonal from the top of the first stroke.

This starts like the "c," but the second stroke is a diagonal beginning on the ascender line, curving minimally to touch the first stroke, but ending on the top of the x height. Finish with a connecting vertical.

The Gothic "e" also starts like the "c." Take the second stroke from the top of the first with a small diagonal to match the lower one, ending with a hairline back into the body of the letter.

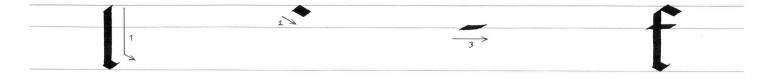

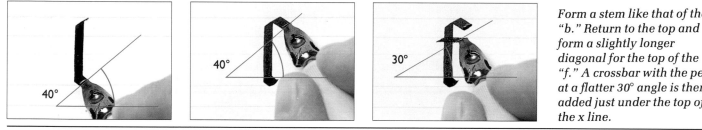

Form a stem like that of the "b." Return to the top and form a slightly longer diagonal for the top of the "f." A crossbar with the pen at a flatter 30° angle is then added just under the top of the x line.

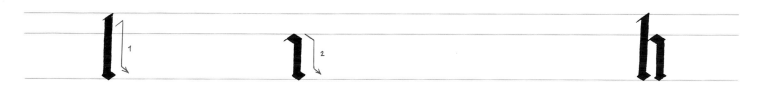

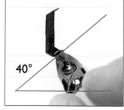
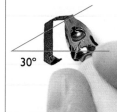
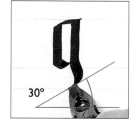
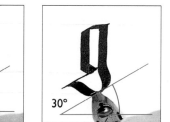

Begin like the "c," then add a small curved horizontal line with the pen at 30°. Moving from within this stroke to the base line, curve gently right and left. End with a flourish joining the first and third strokes.

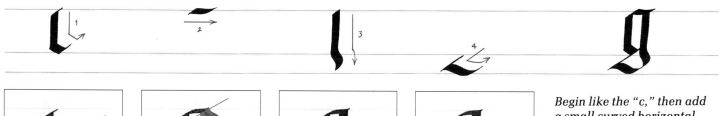

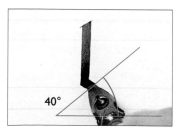
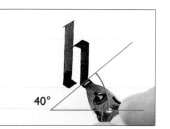

The letter "h" begins like the "b" with a line serif on the ascender line and then continues vertically toward the base line, stopping just short before changing to a small diagonal. With the left edge of the nib touching the stem and the right edge the x line, form the second stroke as a small diagonal before dropping vertically to finish with a diagonal foot in a diamond shape touching the base line.

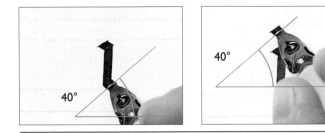

Begin the letter "i" with a very short diagonal stroke to form a diamond on the top of the x height, then continue vertically down to just before the base line where the stroke changes back to a diagonal. These small diagonals, or shoulders and feet, are diamond shaped and should balance each other. The dot is a minimal diagonal stroke forming a diamond immediately over the letter.

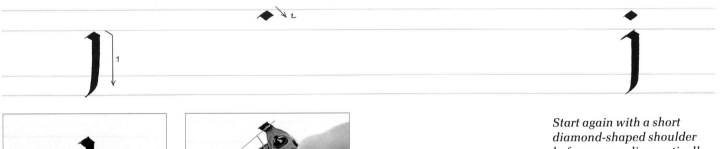

Start again with a short diamond-shaped shoulder before proceeding vertically to just below the base line. Finish the stroke with a small left-hand hairline serif. The dot is a short diamond over the letter.

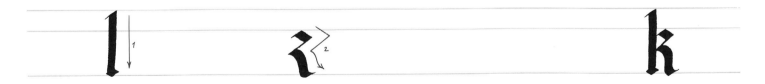

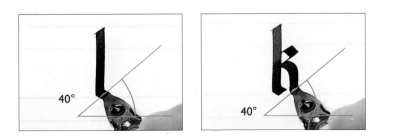

The first stroke is like the letter "h." The second stroke starts with a small diagonal, but then returns with a thin line back into the stem before continuing with a curved diagonal to the base line.

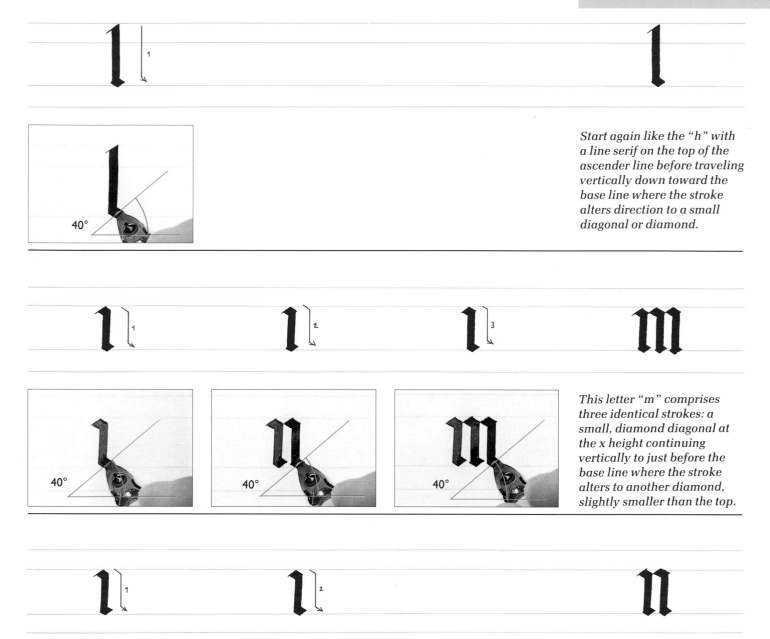

Start again like the "h" with a line serif on the top of the ascender line before traveling vertically down toward the base line where the stroke alters direction to a small diagonal or diamond.

This letter "m" comprises three identical strokes: a small, diamond diagonal at the x height continuing vertically to just before the base line where the stroke alters to another diamond, slightly smaller than the top.

The letter "n" follows the "m" for the first two strokes: a small diagonal proceeding vertically to another diagonal diamond on the base line.

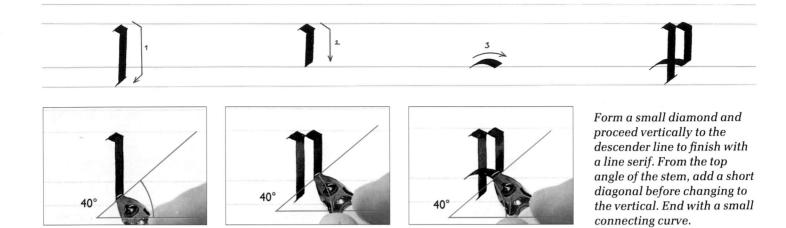

Form a small diamond and proceed vertically to the descender line to finish with a line serif. From the top angle of the stem, add a short diagonal before changing to the vertical. End with a small connecting curve.

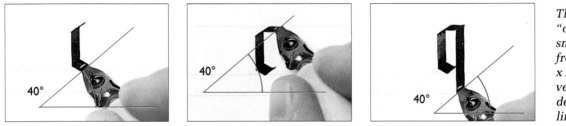

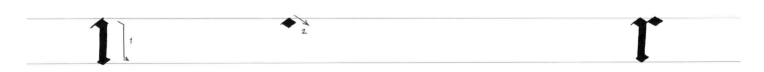

The letter "q" starts like the "o." The second stroke is a small horizontal running from the top of the first at the x height. Finish with a vertical stroke to the descender line, ending with a line serif.

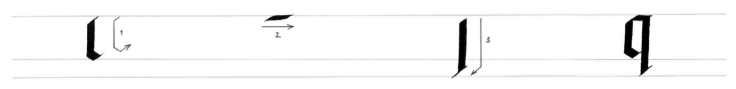

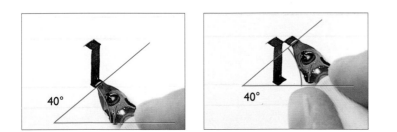

Construct the letter "r" out of one of the strokes of the "m." Then, returning to the top, add another small diagonal diamond to the right of the first stroke.

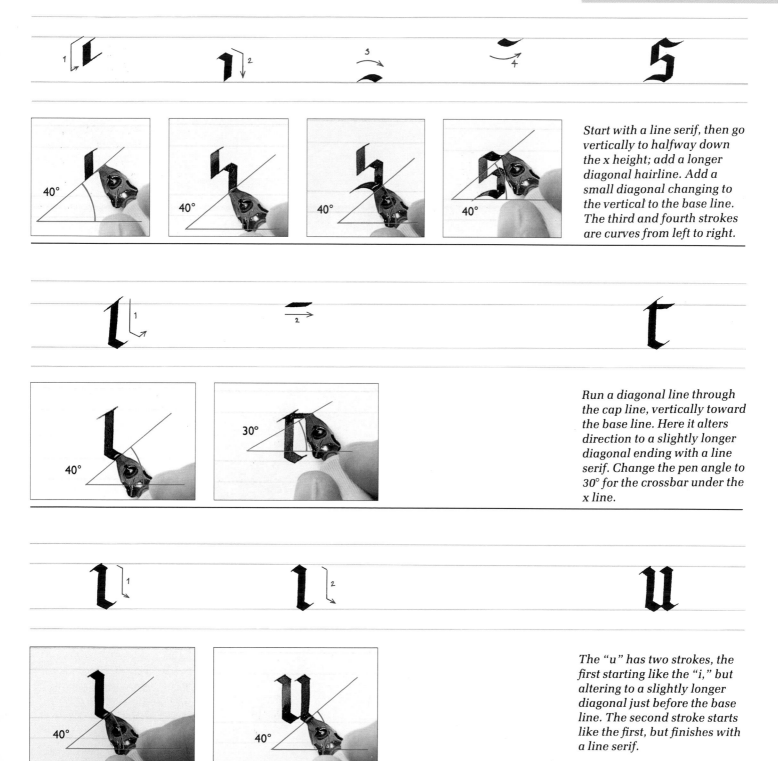

Start with a line serif, then go vertically to halfway down the x height; add a longer diagonal hairline. Add a small diagonal changing to the vertical to the base line. The third and fourth strokes are curves from left to right.

Run a diagonal line through the cap line, vertically toward the base line. Here it alters direction to a slightly longer diagonal ending with a line serif. Change the pen angle to 30° for the crossbar under the x line.

The "u" has two strokes, the first starting like the "i," but altering to a slightly longer diagonal just before the base line. The second stroke starts like the first, but finishes with a line serif.

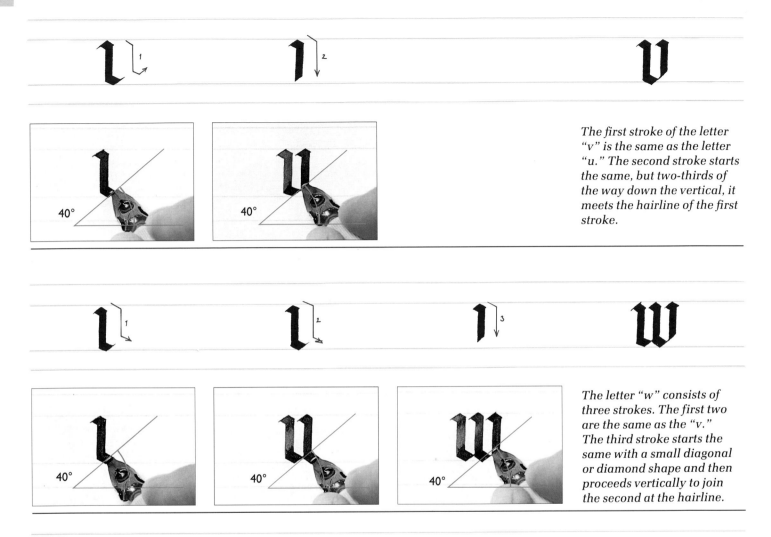

The first stroke of the letter "v" is the same as the letter "u." The second stroke starts the same, but two-thirds of the way down the vertical, it meets the hairline of the first stroke.

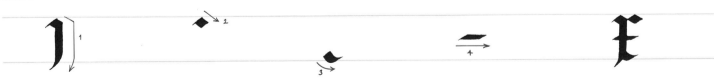

The letter "w" consists of three strokes. The first two are the same as the "v." The third stroke starts the same with a small diagonal or diamond shape and then proceeds vertically to join the second at the hairline.

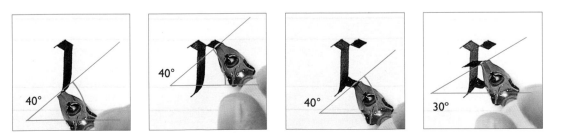

Start as with "j," ending just below the base line. Add a diamond at the top to the right, and a small curve to the right of the stem at the base line, tapering to a hairline. Change to 30° for a horizontal central crossbar.

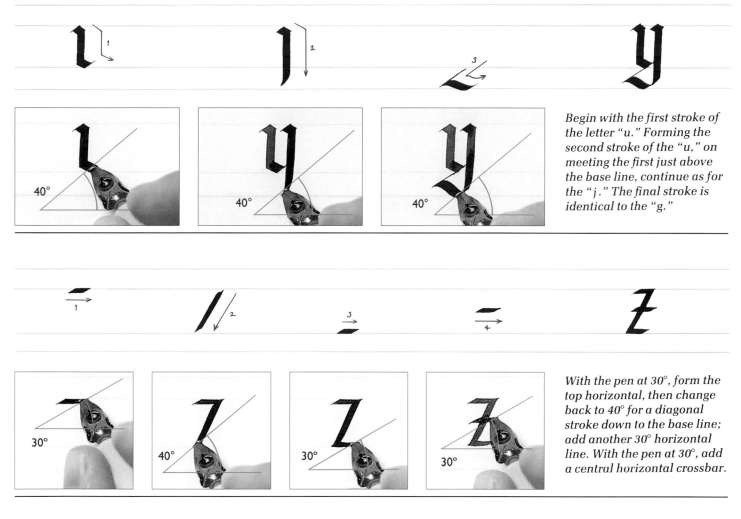

Begin with the first stroke of the letter "u." Forming the second stroke of the "u," on meeting the first just above the base line, continue as for the "j." The final stroke is identical to the "g."

With the pen at 30°, form the top horizontal, then change back to 40° for a diagonal stroke down to the base line; add another 30° horizontal line. With the pen at 30°, add a central horizontal crossbar.

ALTERNATIVES

Gothic lower-case alternatives should be consistent throughout a piece of work. So if you use small diagonal serifs at the top of ascenders of the "b," "h," "k," and "l" and at the bottom of "p" and "q," they should be uniform throughout.

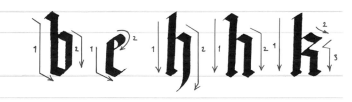

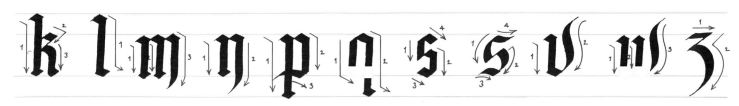

Troubleshooting

As the Gothic lower case depends so much on the rhythm and inner textured appearance of the letters, it is all the more important to keep all verticals as straight as you can and all inner spaces equal. With the letter "m," for instance, both sides must be kept balanced with the angle constant at 40°. Take care with the top diagonals of the letters "f" and "r," which should not be too long, or they will not be consistent with the rest of the alphabet.

All the elements of this letter have been constructed with the pen held at far too steep an angle (more than 40°), making the letter too thin.

Correct Letterforms

abcdefghijklm

The letter "a" has been constructed so that there is too much white space inside the letter, making it too wide compared with the rest of the alphabet.

An incorrect downstroke has been used with this letter "d," giving it a very odd appearance.

The top of the letter "f" has been constructed with too long a diagonal. The horizontal crossbar is also too far down the stem and needs to come just under the x line.

The letter "m" is not balanced because the second inner area is too wide.

The top counter space of the letter "e" is far too small and looks as if it is closing up. In addition, the bottom diagonal is too long.

The counter space of this letter "p" is too large.

In contrast, the counter space of this letter is too small.

This letter "z" has been constructed with the pen at the wrong angle, which makes the horizontal strokes far too narrow.

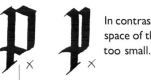

n o p q r s t u v w x y z

The second stroke, the diagonal arm of the letter "r," is far too long, and you can see that the letter does not look very balanced.

The counter spaces of the letter "w" are not equal, the second space being much too wide.

The crossbar of the letter "t" is too low and too narrow.

CAPITALS

Gothic capitals are impressive yet decorative letters. They are best used on their own, since when they are written in a complete word, such as in a heading, they can become difficult to read. There are many variations of these letters with extra added hairlines and diamond shapes which can add to their appeal. This alphabet is much more curved than the lowercase version. It is made up of generous curves to letters such as the "O," "E," and "G" with tapered ends to vertical lines. Distinctive sharp "teeth" are added to the main strokes of some letters. These capitals should not be constructed too tall, or they lose their characteristic roundness.

Most of the Gothic capital letters consist of several letter strokes, like the letters "M" and "W," for example, so extra care should be taken during the construction sequence. After practicing the capital letters for a while, the same rhythm as with the lowercase Gothic letters can be achieved, which gives great pleasure to writing a set piece of lettering when the style is mastered.

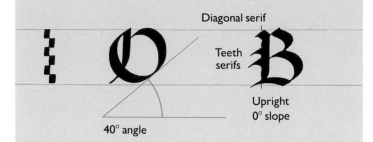

ESSENTIAL INFORMATION

Diagonal serif
Teeth serifs
Upright 0° slope
40° angle

Letter height The x height for this alphabet is 6 nib widths.
Basic pen angle The pen angle for most letters is 40°. However, the angle is flattened to 30° for the crossbars.
"O" form Circular.
Slope This is an upright alphabet.
Serif form Small line serifs, small diagonal serifs, and decorative "teeth" serifs are a feature of this alphabet.
Letter groups As the letters in this alphabet are so individual, it does not really have letter groups. However, the following letters are related to the "O" form: "C," "E," "G," and "Q."

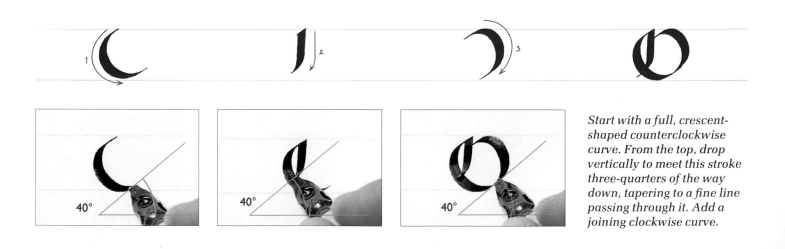

Start with a full, crescent-shaped counterclockwise curve. From the top, drop vertically to meet this stroke three-quarters of the way down, tapering to a fine line passing through it. Add a joining clockwise curve.

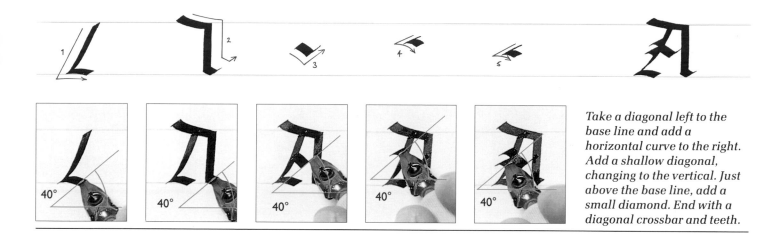

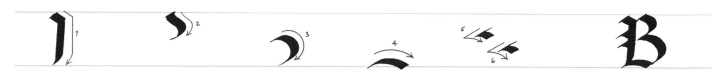

Take a diagonal left to the base line and add a horizontal curve to the right. Add a shallow diagonal, changing to the vertical. Just above the base line, add a small diamond. End with a diagonal crossbar and teeth.

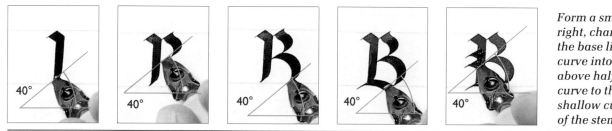

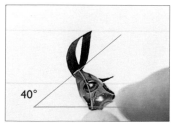
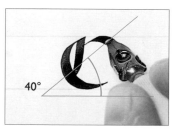

Form a small diagonal to the right, changing vertically to the base line. At the top, curve into the letter just above halfway. From here, curve to the base line. Add a shallow curve from the base of the stem, and two teeth.

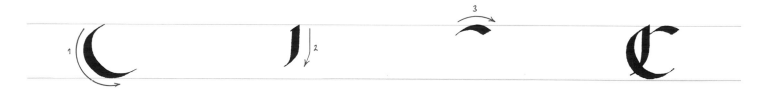

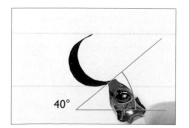

Start with the crescent of the "O." Then add a vertical from the top, curving back into it three-quarters of the way down. Finish with an arc from just below the top of the second stroke, ending in a sheared terminal.

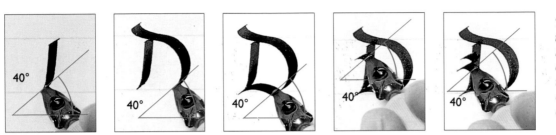

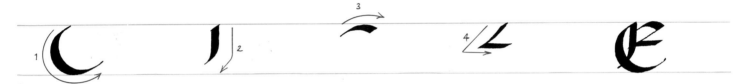

Take a vertical stroke from the cap line to the base line. Start above the cap line and curve slightly to the left; on the cap line, straighten before curving to the base line. Add a shallow curve and teeth.

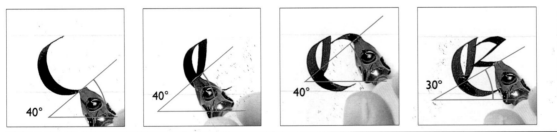

The first three strokes of the letter "E" are the same as the "C." The last stroke is a crossbar from the base of the third stroke with the pen at an angle of 30°.

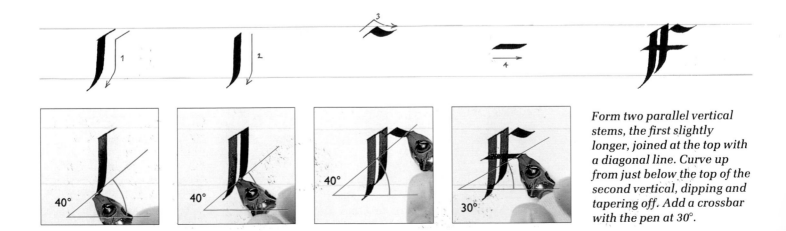

Form two parallel vertical stems, the first slightly longer, joined at the top with a diagonal line. Curve up from just below the top of the second vertical, dipping and tapering off. Add a crossbar with the pen at 30°.

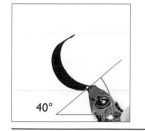 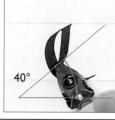 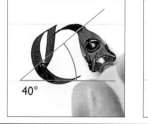 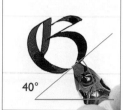

Form the three strokes of "C" or "E." The fourth stroke joins the first and third strokes with a fine line diagonal, followed by a generous clockwise curve to join the first stroke.

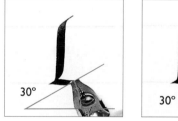 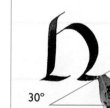 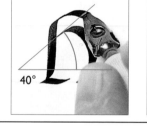 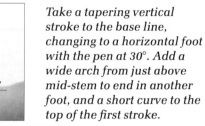

Take a tapering vertical stroke to the base line, changing to a horizontal foot with the pen at 30°. Add a wide arch from just above mid-stem to end in another foot, and a short curve to the top of the first stroke.

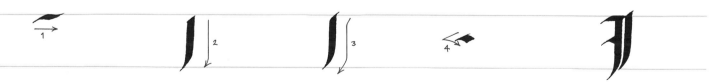

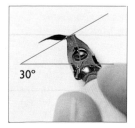 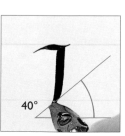 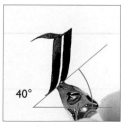 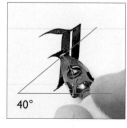

A small wave stroke just below the cap line begins the letter "I." Now form the main stem with two vertical strokes ending with slight kicks to the left, the first slightly longer. One decorative tooth is then added.

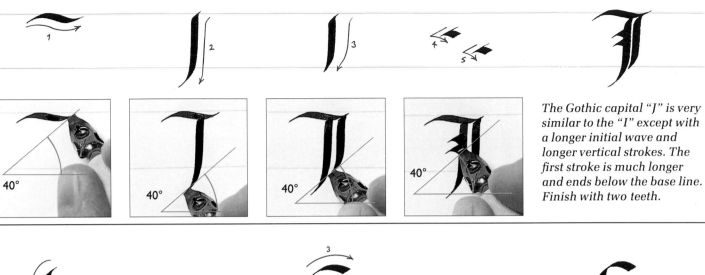

The Gothic capital "J" is very similar to the "I" except with a longer initial wave and longer vertical strokes. The first stroke is much longer and ends below the base line. Finish with two teeth.

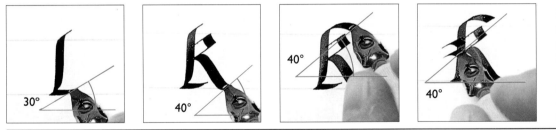

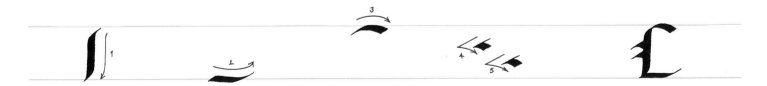

Drop from above the cap line toward the base line to change to a horizontal foot with the pen at 30°. Add the "bowl" from within the letter: a thin line upward, a diagonal, another thin line, and a longer diagonal foot.

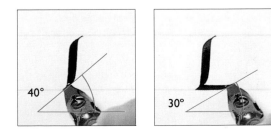
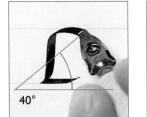
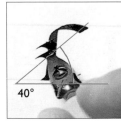

Form a vertical downstroke, starting and ending with a tapered kick from right to left. Change to 30° for a horizontal, tapering to a fine line. Curve from the top of the vertical, ending with a sheared terminal.

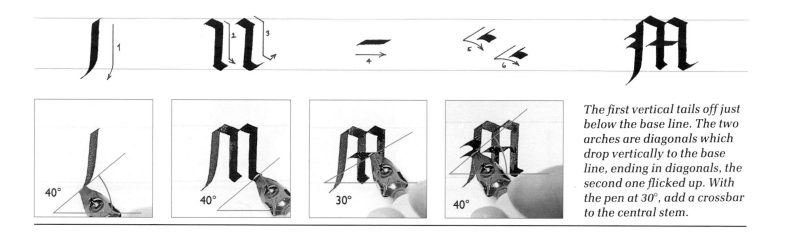

The first vertical tails off just below the base line. The two arches are diagonals which drop vertically to the base line, ending in diagonals, the second one flicked up. With the pen at 30°, add a crossbar to the central stem.

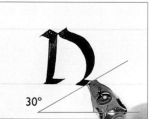
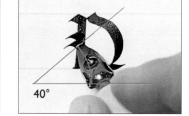
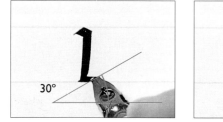
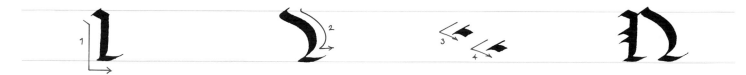

Form a short diagonal dropping vertically to the base line, where the pen is turned to 30° for a horizontal foot. Add a hairline from the top of the first stroke, curving left and right to the base line; add another 30° foot.

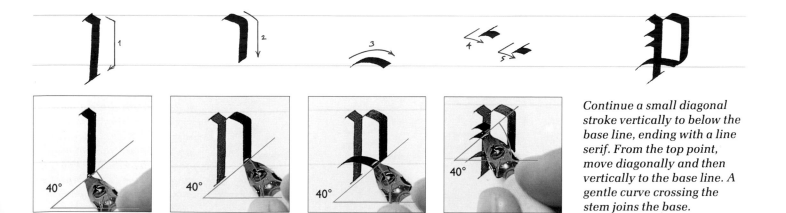

Continue a small diagonal stroke vertically to below the base line, ending with a line serif. From the top point, move diagonally and then vertically to the base line. A gentle curve crossing the stem joins the base.

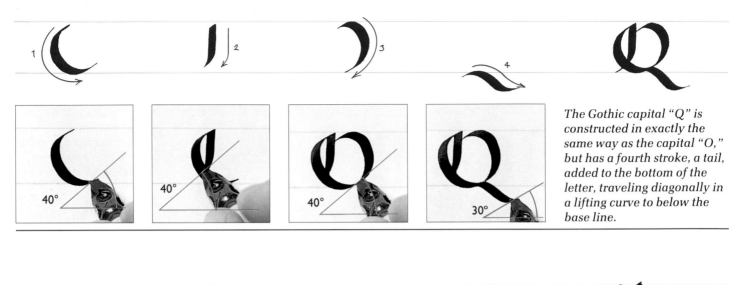

The Gothic capital "Q" is constructed in exactly the same way as the capital "O," but has a fourth stroke, a tail, added to the bottom of the letter, traveling diagonally in a lifting curve to below the base line.

Start with the first stroke of the letter "N." Add a hairline from the top joint, curving into the body of the letter just below halfway. From this point, form the diagonal curve to the base line and add two teeth.

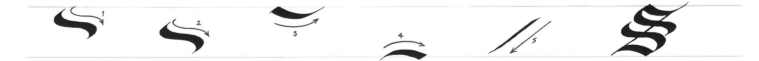

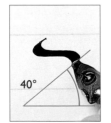
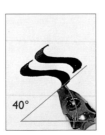
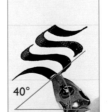
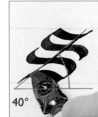

Make two parallel S-shaped strokes, one above the other on a slight diagonal. Add long, shallow, tapered curves, for the top and base. Then run a thin diagonal from top to bottom through the middle of the letter.

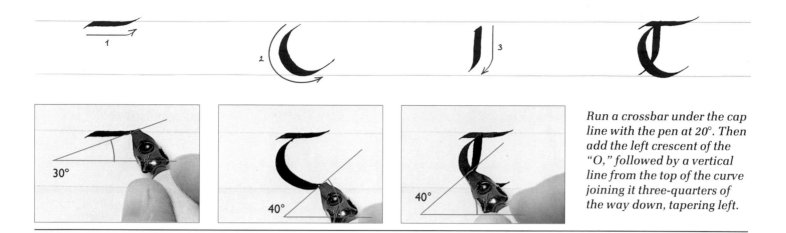

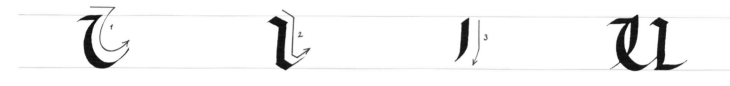

Run a crossbar under the cap line with the pen at 20°. Then add the left crescent of the "O," followed by a vertical line from the top of the curve joining it three-quarters of the way down, tapering left.

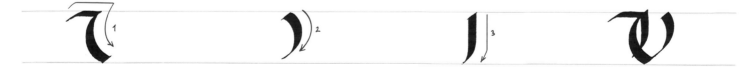

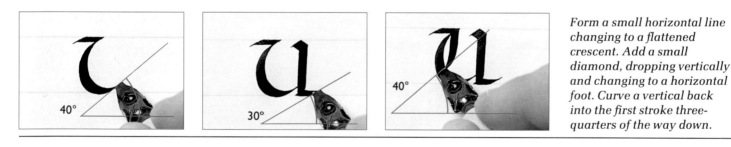

Form a small horizontal line changing to a flattened crescent. Add a small diamond, dropping vertically and changing to a horizontal foot. Curve a vertical back into the first stroke three-quarters of the way down.

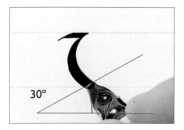
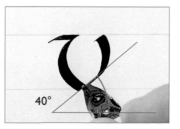
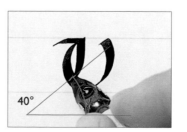

With the pen at 30°, form a small horizontal line which then curves to the base line. Don't make it too deep. Add a clockwise curve joining this stroke at the base. Now arch a vertical back into the first curve halfway down.

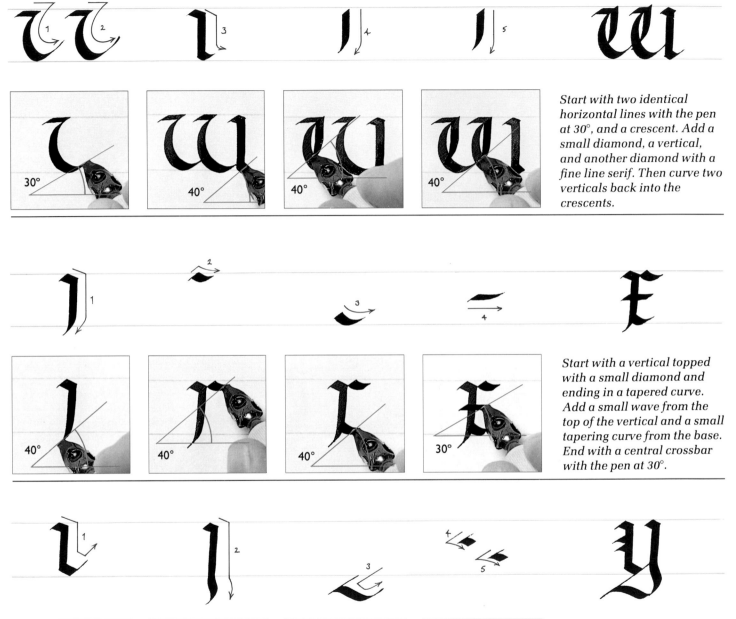

Start with two identical horizontal lines with the pen at 30°, and a crescent. Add a small diamond, a vertical, and another diamond with a fine line serif. Then curve two verticals back into the crescents.

Start with a vertical topped with a small diamond and ending in a tapered curve. Add a small wave from the top of the vertical and a small tapering curve from the base. End with a central crossbar with the pen at 30°.

Take a diagonal vertically toward the base line to change to a longer diagonal ending with a thin line. Add a small diagonal changing vertically to taper to the right. Now join the bases of the first and second strokes.

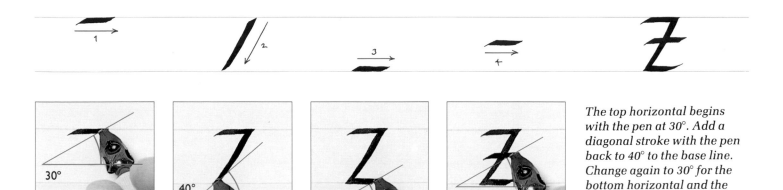

The top horizontal begins with the pen at 30°. Add a diagonal stroke with the pen back to 40° to the base line. Change again to 30° for the bottom horizontal and the central crossbar to finish.

ALTERNATIVES

There are probably more alternative Gothic capital letters than any other alphabet. However, as with all alternatives, make sure they are used consistently. If an alternative 'O' is chosen, for example, similar letters, like the "C," "E," "G," and "Q" should match. Punctuation marks and numbers should be in character with the rest of the alphabet, either ranged, making them all the same height as the capital letters, or non-ranged and used with the lower-case letters.

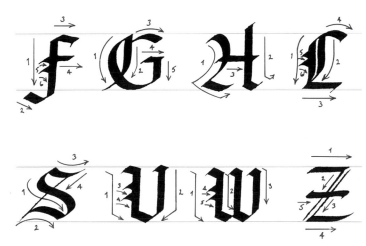

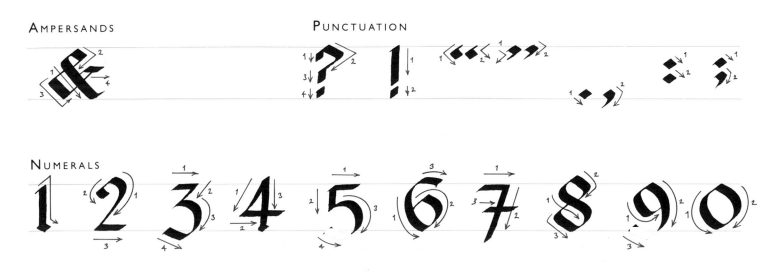

AMPERSANDS

PUNCTUATION

NUMERALS

TROUBLESHOOTING

As Gothic capitals are so decorative, they look as if they are complicated to construct. Indeed, it is easy to get confused with pen angles and balancing the letters, making some too narrow or too heavy. It is important to practise the curves of letters "O," "C," "E," and "Q," keeping them consistent. Also check that the vertical downstrokes are parallel. Finally, make sure that the inner spaces of letters with a repeated shape, such as "S" and "M," are equal.

The two vertical downstrokes of the letter "J" are too close together.

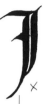

CORRECT LETTERFORMS

ABCDEFGHIJKLM

The top counter space of this letter is too big which, as you can see, makes the letter appear top-heavy.

The crossbar of this letter "E" has been added too low down, which makes it look as if it is dropping down into the curve.

The main elements of this letter have been constructed too close together. It may help to map it out in pencil first until the spacing comes naturally.

This letter is not balanced because the counter area is too small and too high up the letter.

The inside area (counter) of this letter "N" is too small because the letter has been constructed too close together.

The two central parallel curves of this Gothic "S" are far too close together, which makes it look too heavy.

In this second letter "S," the central parallel curves are too far apart, making the top section look as if it is drifting away.

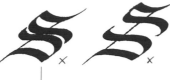

NOPQRSTUVWXYZ

The vertical downstroke of this letter is too much in the center of the letter. It should be taken down from the top of the curve, rejoining it with a slow, tapering curve to the left.

The pen has been held at too steep an angle for the horizontal line of this letter, making it look top-heavy.

The incorrect angle was held for the whole of this letter "Q". This makes it look out of place and far too thick and heavy.

GALLERY

Gothic lettering always gives the impression of being a very strong and dramatic style. The examples shown on these pages give very different approaches to the overall effect of the work, first through a more harmonious feel using tones of watercolor, then with a piece full of life and vitality incorporating many flourishes. The gallery includes a bold piece of Shakespeare featuring a contrast between Gothic lettering and small Roman capitals.

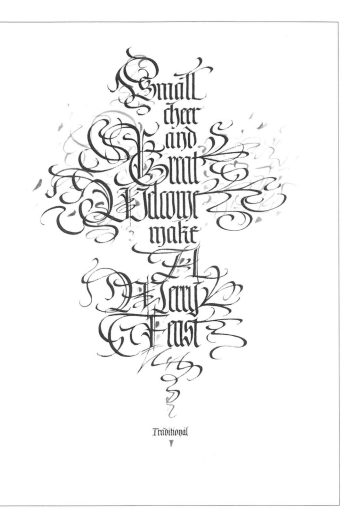

Traditional

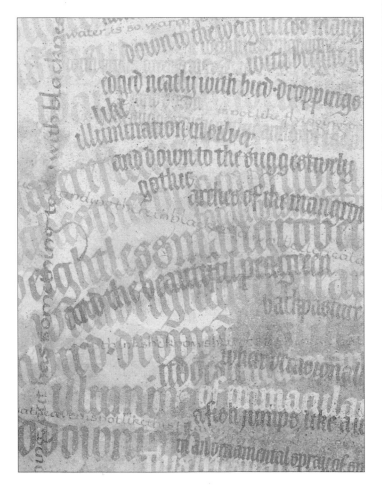

◀ **LIGHTHOUSE (DETAIL)**
Here Barbara J. Bruene has used many layers of Gothic lower-case letters inspired by Seascape by Elizabeth Bishop, which are an important feature of this work. The effect is of a textured and woven appearance, with lines being written in various directions. It has been achieved with steel nibs by the use of subtle variations of watercolor with gouache then added to give more contrast.

▲ **TRADITIONAL**
This work by Jenny Hunter Groat may live up to its title, but it is also a refreshing and energetic work of Gothic lettering written in black ink in various sizes. The highly decorative capitals have been combined with the use of free-flowing flourishes, which include brightly colored embellishments, giving the whole text a lively feel.

▶ HAMLET

Annie Moring's imaginative interpretation from Shakespeare's Hamlet has been created on Saunders Waterford HP paper using acrylic inks for the background effects. The Gothic text has deliberately been written much taller in black ink using metal nibs. In between each line and repeating the text are small Roman capitals written in red gouache with a quill. The experimental heading, which is in total contrast to the rest of the text, has been written with a ruling pen and balances all the techniques perfectly.

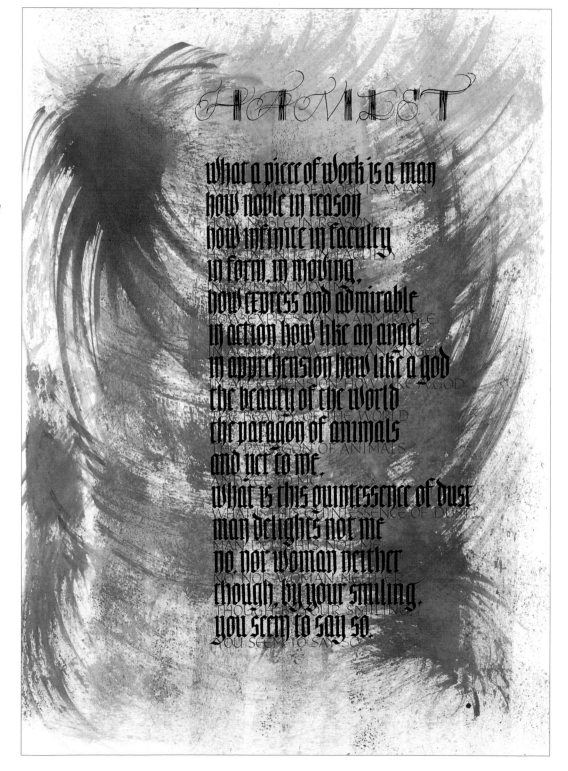

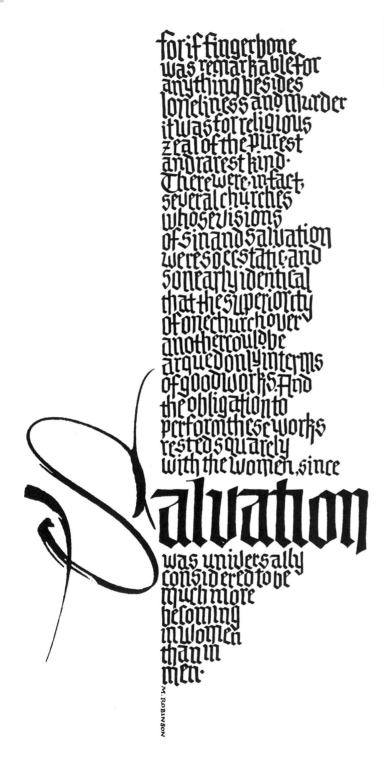

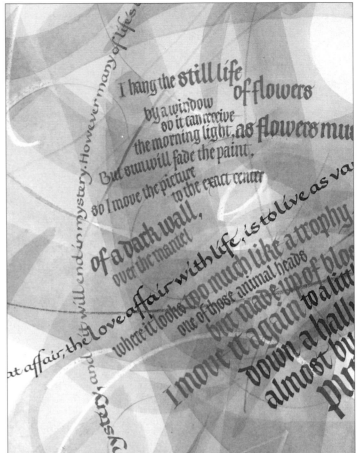

◀ SALVATION

This very balanced piece of Gothic lettering has been achieved even though the letters have been constructed irregularly, showing that great thought has been given to the overall layout. In contrast, the title gives a strong impact to the work, with the capital "S" drawn freely using a ruling pen. The rest of the text was written by Cheryl Jacobsen using metal nibs in gouache and water-color on Arches HP paper.

▲ STILL LIFE (DETAIL)

Many techniques have been used by Barbara J. Bruene in this piece of work, including various Gothic letter sizes written in gouache colors on an interesting background of wax oil crayons and colored pencils. The text has been chosen from several sources, including The Myth of Perfectability *by Linda Pastan and* A Natural History of the Senses *by Diane Ackerman.*

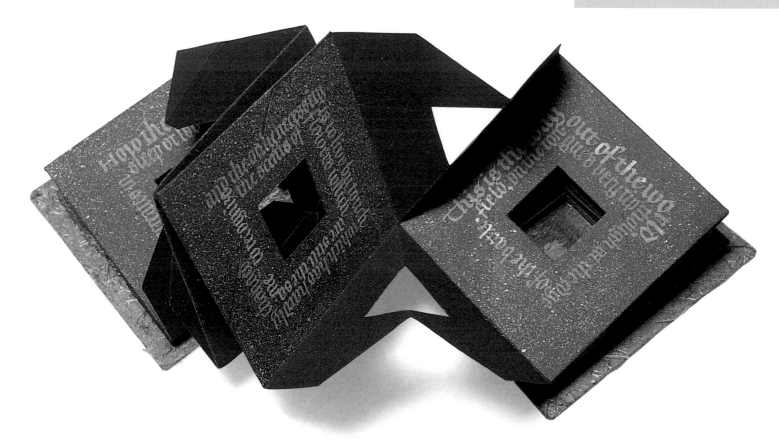

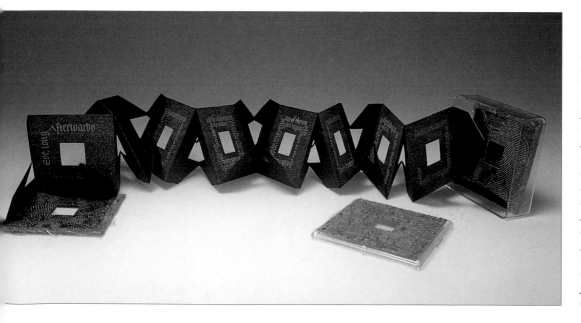

▶▲ EVE: HONEY IN A BOX
The calligrapher of this work, Barbara J. Bruene, has used an ingenious and exciting way of presenting poetry, using Gothic lettering, from a poem Eve, Long Afterwards by Linda Pastan, and is of great inspiration to others. A combination of handmade and machine-made papers has been used, including silver mylar, and various gouache paints. As you can see from the second photograph, the whole work can be extended to 40 inches, and, when closed, the finished piece is presented in a recycled plastic box.

ITALIC CURSIVE

Italic cursive is based on the traditional italic oval script, but it has been developed into a modern free-flowing style of writing much used by calligraphers today. This is a versatile hand which can be written at great speed. Entire words and lines can be stretched out to dance across the page, making it ideal for poetry and prose.

Italic cursive is a lower-case alphabet with oval shapes, springing arches, and very few pen lifts. Fine diagonal ligatures join the letters together, giving the alphabet more rhythm and movement than other styles. Small oval serifs and a gentle forward slope add to its grace and beauty.

Although the example alphabet shown in this section is of the lower-case letters, the same treatment can be used for the Italic capital letters. Making them deliberately joined combined with the increased writing speed allows the calligrapher greater creativity. Both lower- and upper-case Italic cursive letters benefit from extended ascenders and descenders, including the use of well-constructed flourishes. Poetry and prose look particularly appealing using several lines of Italic cursive lower case followed by a section of just capital letters as a contrast, proceeding again with lower-case letters.

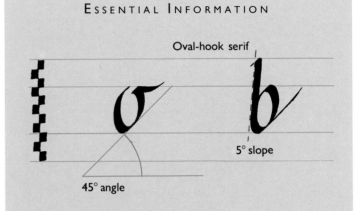

ESSENTIAL INFORMATION

Oval-hook serif

5° slope

45° angle

Letter height The x height is 5 nib widths, with ascenders and descenders extending an extra 3 nib widths.
Basic pen angle Usually 45°, with 20° used for crossbars.
"O" form Oval.
Slope Letters may have a forward slant of between 5° and 10°.
Serif forms Small oval-hook serifs echoing the oval "o" are used.
Letter groups These groups are exactly the same as for the Italic minuscule alphabet (see page 44).

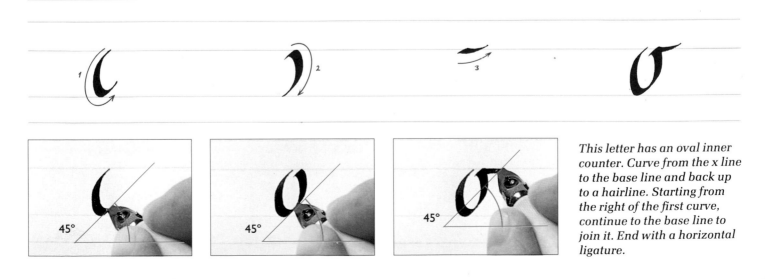

1   2   3

45°   45°   45°

This letter has an oval inner counter. Curve from the x line to the base line and back up to a hairline. Starting from the right of the first curve, continue to the base line to join it. End with a horizontal ligature.

Start as for the letter "o," then add shallow curve for the top arch. From here, drop vertically to the base line then curve the stroke around to form a thin diagonal ligature so that other letters can be adjoined.

Start with a small oval-hook serif on the ascender line, continuing to the base line to curve back up in a wide oval serif. Form a right-hand curve to join the hairline of this serif and add a diagonal ligature from the base line.

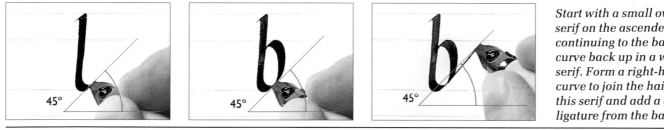

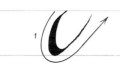

The Italic "c" is a typical oval, starting with a gentle counterclockwise curve to the base line and then back up to form a fine diagonal ligature up to the x height. A small flattened curve forms the top of the letter.

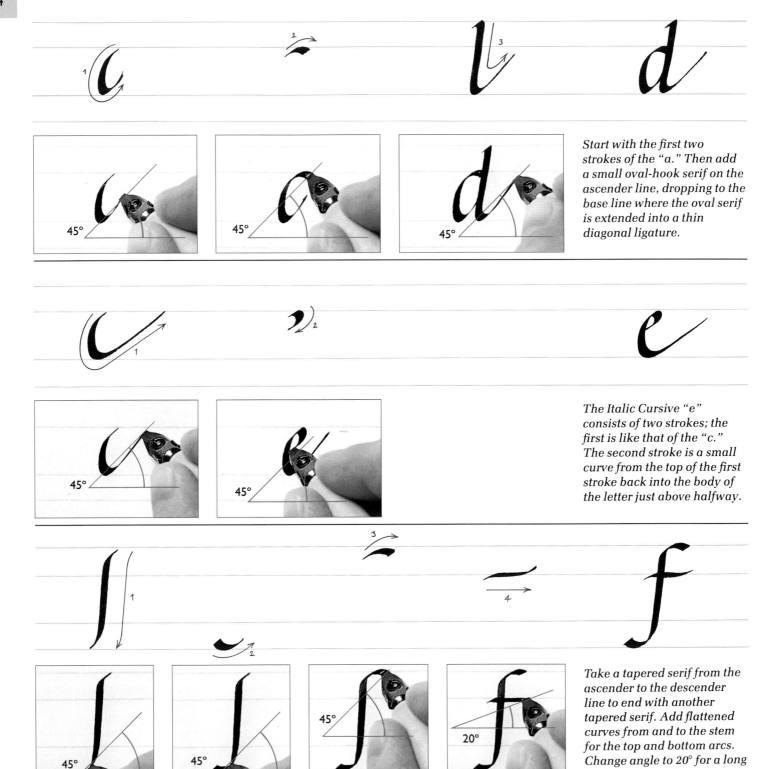

Start with the first two strokes of the "a." Then add a small oval-hook serif on the ascender line, dropping to the base line where the oval serif is extended into a thin diagonal ligature.

The Italic Cursive "e" consists of two strokes; the first is like that of the "c." The second stroke is a small curve from the top of the first stroke back into the body of the letter just above halfway.

Take a tapered serif from the ascender to the descender line to end with another tapered serif. Add flattened curves from and to the stem for the top and bottom arcs. Change angle to 20° for a long horizontal crossbar.

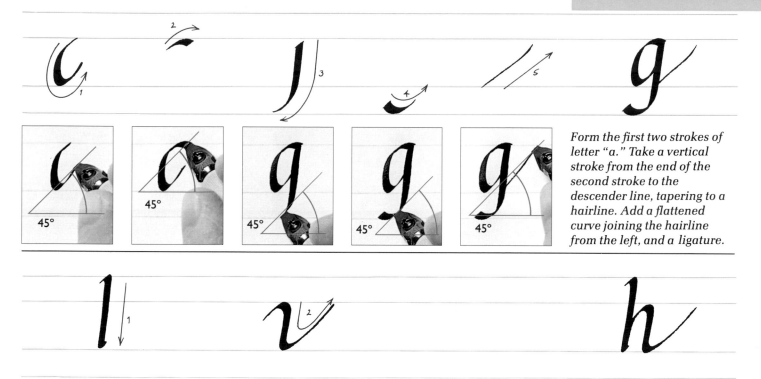

Form the first two strokes of letter "a." Take a vertical stroke from the end of the second stroke to the descender line, tapering to a hairline. Add a flattened curve joining the hairline from the left, and a ligature.

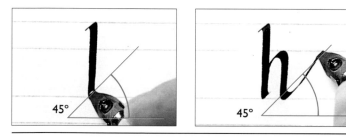

Start the letter "h" with a small oval-hook serif on the top of the ascender line coming down to a similar oval-hook serif to the right on the base line. The second stroke springs from the base of the stem, leaving it just above halfway to arch down to the base line before curving back up into a diagonal ligature extended to the top of the x height.

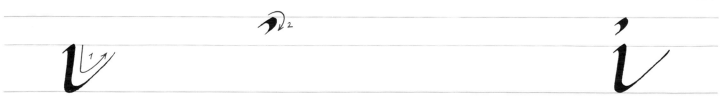

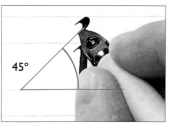

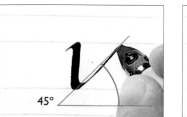

The first stroke begins with a small oval-hook serif from the x line, continuing down to the base line where it curves back up, tapering to a thin diagonal ligature. The dot is a small oval curve over the letter.

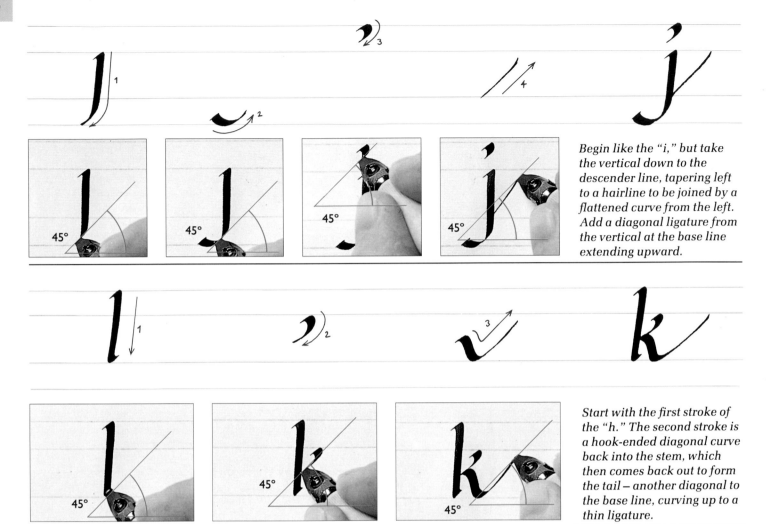

Begin like the "i," but take the vertical down to the descender line, tapering left to a hairline to be joined by a flattened curve from the left. Add a diagonal ligature from the vertical at the base line extending upward.

Start with the first stroke of the "h." The second stroke is a hook-ended diagonal curve back into the stem, which then comes back out to form the tail – another diagonal to the base line, curving up to a thin ligature.

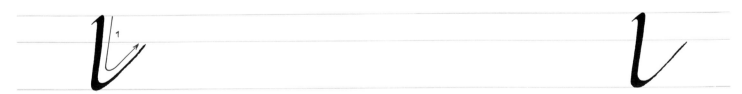

The letter "l" begins at the top of the ascender line with a small oval-hook serif proceeding to the base line with a 5° slope to the vertical. Then it curves back up, tapering to a thin ligature.

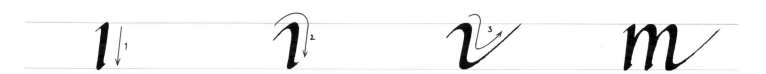

Form an oval-hook serif, then run it down to the base line, ending with another serif. From the base of the stems, leave just above halfway to arch around and down. Curve the third stroke up to form the ligature.

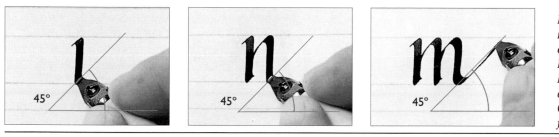

Construct the first stroke of the "m." The second springs from the base of the stem, leaving it halfway up, then arches before dropping to the base line. It then curves back up to form the ligature.

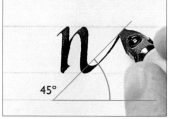

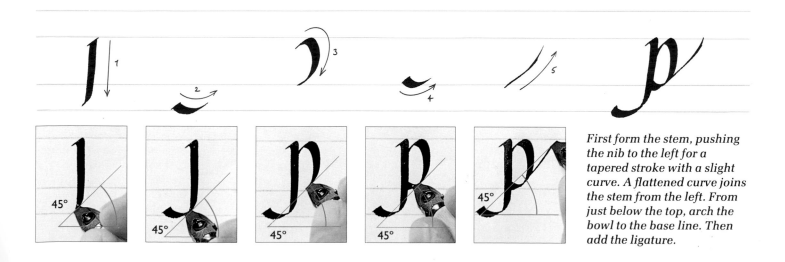

First form the stem, pushing the nib to the left for a tapered stroke with a slight curve. A flattened curve joins the stem from the left. From just below the top, arch the bowl to the base line. Then add the ligature.

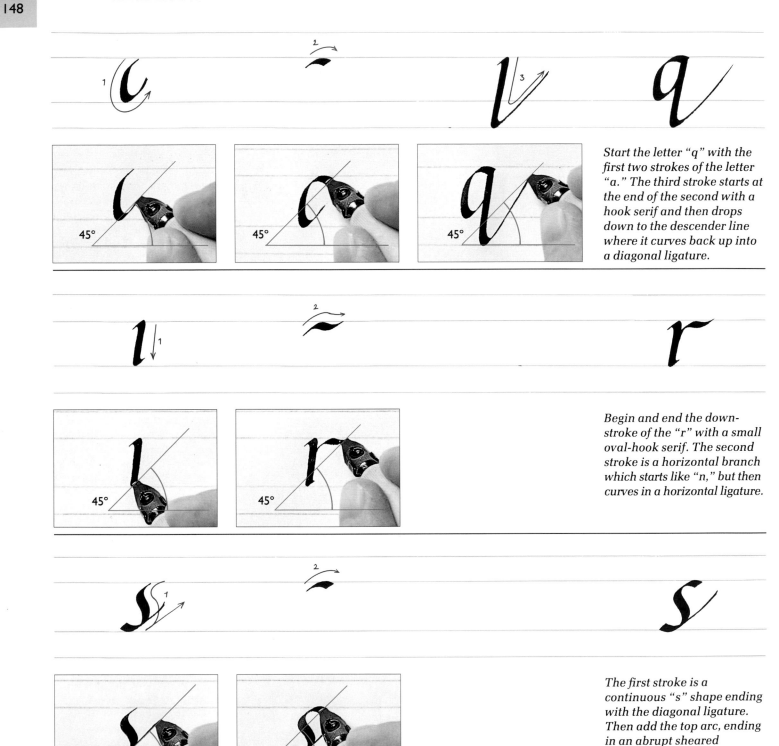

Start the letter "q" with the first two strokes of the letter "a." The third stroke starts at the end of the second with a hook serif and then drops down to the descender line where it curves back up into a diagonal ligature.

Begin and end the downstroke of the "r" with a small oval-hook serif. The second stroke is a horizontal branch which starts like "n," but then curves in a horizontal ligature.

The first stroke is a continuous "s" shape ending with the diagonal ligature. Then add the top arc, ending in an abrupt sheared terminal.

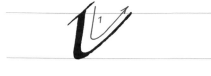

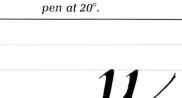

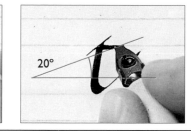

Run a thin diagonal line through the x line. Take a stroke from the middle of this line to the base line where it curves back up in a diagonal ligature. Add a crossbar under the x line, with the pen at 20°.

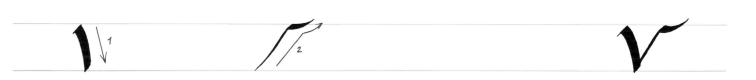

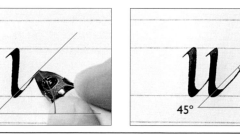

This letter is two strokes, starting with small oval-hook serifs and continuing to the base line before curving up. The second stroke joins the first at the hairline and then curves up to form the ligature.

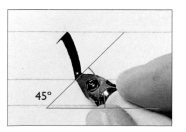

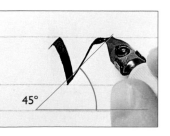

The "v" starts with a strong, slightly curved diagonal down to the base line. The next stroke starts on the base line and travels diagonally up to the x line, ending with a small horizontal flag serif.

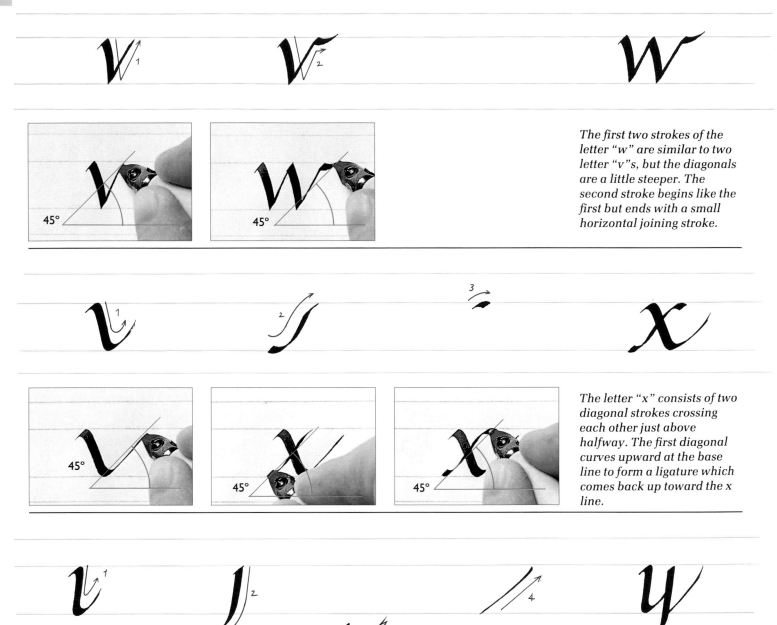

The first two strokes of the letter "w" are similar to two letter "v"s, but the diagonals are a little steeper. The second stroke begins like the first but ends with a small horizontal joining stroke.

The letter "x" consists of two diagonal strokes crossing each other just above halfway. The first diagonal curves upward at the base line to form a ligature which comes back up toward the x line.

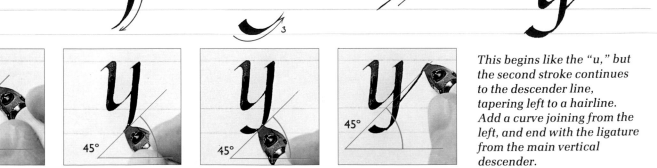

This begins like the "u," but the second stroke continues to the descender line, tapering left to a hairline. Add a curve joining from the left, and end with the ligature from the main vertical descender.

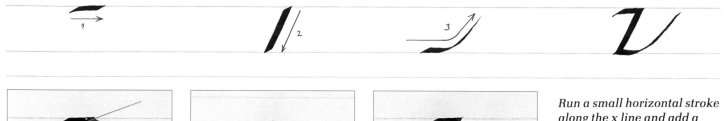

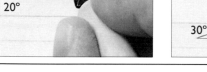

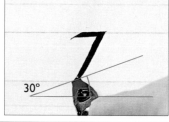

Run a small horizontal stroke along the x line and add a diagonal from the end of this stroke to the base line. The final stroke starts along the base line at 20°, but then curves up to form the ligature with the pen at 45°.

ALTERNATIVES

Alternative forms of Italic cursive are similar to the Italic lower case, but joins should be added to connect them with other letters. Numbers are the same height and oval shape as the rest of the alphabet and can be joined in a similar way to the letters if this is part of the design. Punctuation is also in keeping with the alphabet shape.

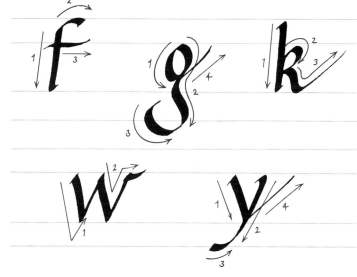

AMPERSANDS

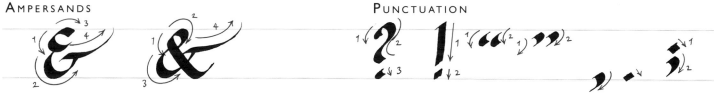

PUNCTUATION

NUMERALS

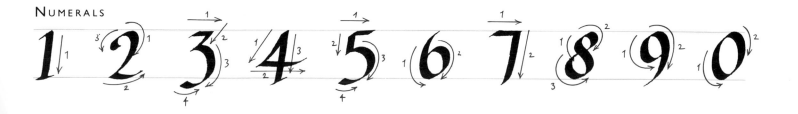

TROUBLESHOOTING

Because Italic cursive letters are joined together almost all at the same angle, it is important to make sure they are traveling in the same direction. Horizontal crossbars on letters "t," "f," and "z" should not be too heavy, as this will alter the appearance of the letters and make them look ugly. The inner areas of the letters "m" and "w" should be optically equal and balanced.

The first arch of this example of the letter "m" is too large, creating too much space and making the letter unbalanced.

The second arch of this "m" has been constructed too wide, making the letter unbalanced.

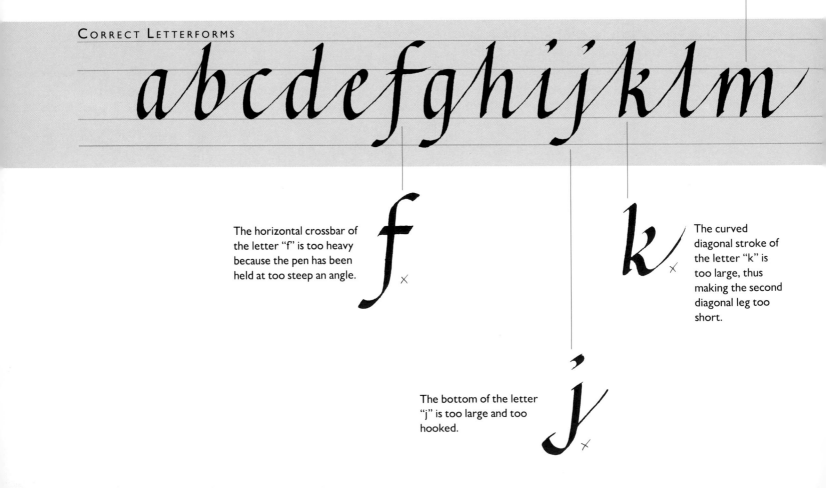

CORRECT LETTERFORMS

The horizontal crossbar of the letter "f" is too heavy because the pen has been held at too steep an angle.

The curved diagonal stroke of the letter "k" is too large, thus making the second diagonal leg too short.

The bottom of the letter "j" is too large and too hooked.

The horizontal crossbar of this "t" is far too heavy because the pen has been held at too steep an angle.

The vertical downstroke of the letter "q" has been executed with the pen held at too flat an angle, making the letter look much too heavy.

The first "v" shape of the letter "w" is too small and therefore does not balance the second.

nopqrstuvwxyz

The top horizontal stroke here is rather heavy and the diagonal stroke far too thin.

The top curve of the letter "s" is too long and the base too small, which makes the letter look as if it is leaning over.

GALLERY

The Italic cursive alphabet lends itself to a rich variety of approaches to both lower-case letters and capitals. In this gallery section, you will see individual calligraphers' ideas on the use of the pen, exploring various ways of altering the height and weights of letters. This in turn reflects the mood of the poetry and prose, and creates energetic and lively finished pieces of artwork. Color, too, has been used in a very subtle manner, including some delicate use of raised gold.

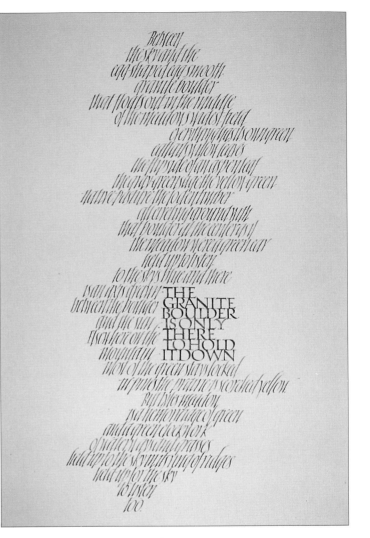

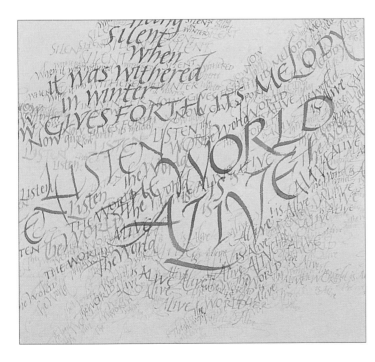

▲ SUMMER'S THRONE (DETAIL)
This free-flowing piece of Italic cursive lettering by Jenny Hunter Groat is an extract from an ancient Gaelic nature poem, written on rag paper in watercolor using both quill and reed pens. Notice how the capitals and lower-case letters intermingle with each other and how vibrant the whole piece of work looks from the effect of using words written on top of each other.

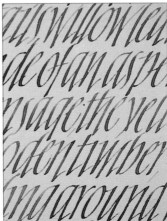

◄▲ THE MEADOW
Here calligrapher Cheryl Jacobsen has chosen a compressed and very slanted Italic cursive style, written quickly using gouache and watercolors, as the detail (left) shows. The layout gives an interesting interpretation to the text The Meadow by James Galvin, particularly in contrast to the Italic and the seven lines toward the end written in Roman capitals.

► BIRD OF PARADISE
This is an exciting example of the use of Italic cursive lettering where the calligrapher, Jenny Hunter Groat, has deliberately incorporated a grass-style feel to the piece using hairline flourishes. This is an ideal way of interpreting the poem by Robert Graves, and this extract has been written on Lana laid rag paper in watercolor using quill pens. Tiny areas of raised and burnished gold complement the work perfectly.

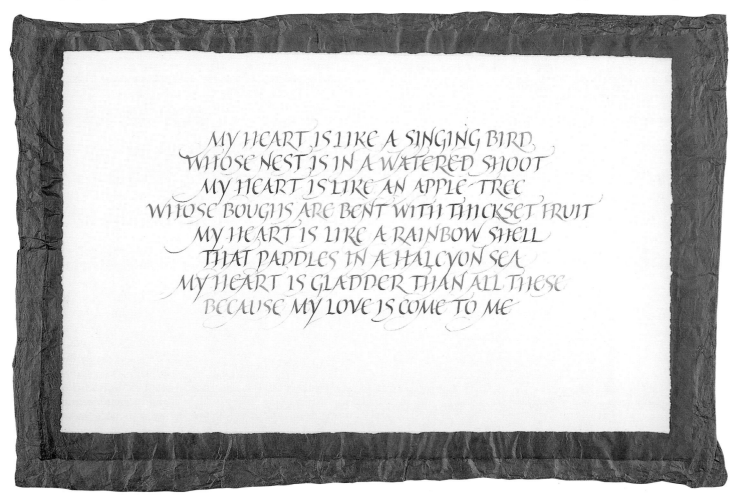

At sunset, only to his true love
The bird of paradise opened wide his wings
Displaying emerald plumage shot with gold
Unguessed even by him. — Robert Graves

BIRD OF PARADISE

True, that wide crest had blazoned royal estate
And the tropic flowers through which he flew
Had shown example of what brave colours gallantly might flaunt
But these were other. She asked herself, trembling,
"What did I do to awake such glory?"

▼ MY HEART IS LIKE A SINGING BIRD
A perfect choice of beautifully arranged and written free-flowing capital letters has been used for this piece of text from A Birthday by Christina Rosetti. The paper used was Saunders Waterford HP with gouache colors, which have been blended in the nib while Sue Gunn was writing. The compressed and flourished letters are finished off with very fine hairline serifs.

MY HEART IS LIKE A SINGING BIRD
WHOSE NEST IS IN A WATERED SHOOT
MY HEART IS LIKE AN APPLE TREE
WHOSE BOUGHS ARE BENT WITH THICKSET FRUIT
MY HEART IS LIKE A RAINBOW SHELL
THAT PADDLES IN A HALCYON SEA
MY HEART IS GLADDER THAN ALL THESE
BECAUSE MY LOVE IS COME TO ME

VERSAL LETTERS

Versals are elegant majuscule letters which were widely used in early illuminated manuscripts, particularly of the 9th and 10th centuries. Versals derived from the Roman *quadrata*, but the thick part of the letters is built up with a number of strokes with a very narrow-edged pen to form the outline, and then this skeleton letter can be filled in with color. Beautiful large versal letters can also be highly decorated, incorporating raised gold leaf in the manner of medieval illuminators. As the name implies, Versals were used to give more emphasis to the beginning of verses, chapters, headings, or even a line of more importance.

Versals can be used in various weights and sizes, and can also be compressed, depending on where the letter is used and its function. The narrow-edge pen is usually held straight, and the letters are drawn rather than written. The vertical stems are very slightly "waisted" with very fine hairline serifs, minimally curved, top and bottom. This gives the letter a graceful and attractive appearance.

ESSENTIAL INFORMATION

0° angle

Hairline serif

Upright 0° slope

Letter height The x height is 24 nib widths.
Basic pen angle The pen angle for this alphabet is a flat 0° angle. The angle changes to 90° for horizontal strokes.
"O" form The inside is oval and the outside circular.
Slope This is an upright alphabet.
Serif forms Very fine hairline serifs are used.
Letter groups The letters "O," "C," "D," "G," and "Q" are circular outside and oval inside. The three-quarter width letters are "A," "H," "N," "T," "U," "V," "X," "Y," and "Z." The following are half width letters: "I," "J," "K," "B," "P," "R," "S," "E," "F," "L." The widest letters are "M" and "W."

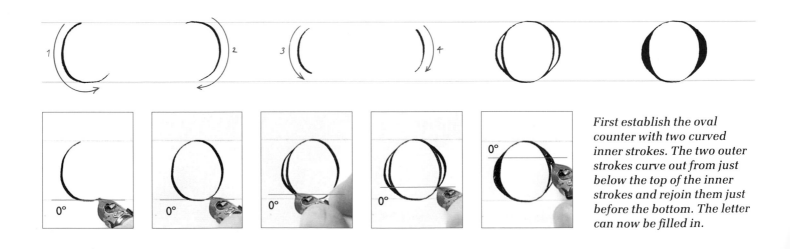

First establish the oval counter with two curved inner strokes. The two outer strokes curve out from just below the top of the inner strokes and rejoin them just before the bottom. The letter can now be filled in.

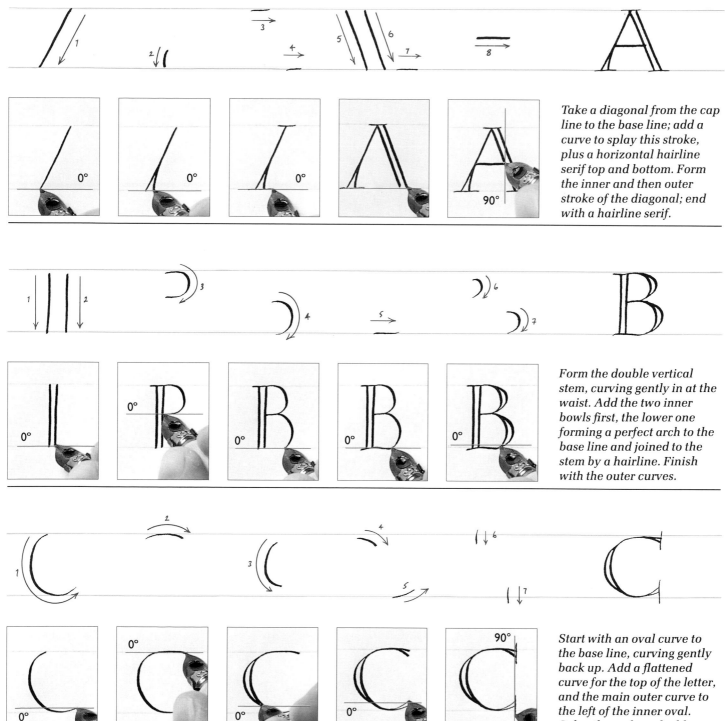

Take a diagonal from the cap line to the base line; add a curve to splay this stroke, plus a horizontal hairline serif top and bottom. Form the inner and then outer stroke of the diagonal; end with a hairline serif.

Form the double vertical stem, curving gently in at the waist. Add the two inner bowls first, the lower one forming a perfect arch to the base line and joined to the stem by a hairline. Finish with the outer curves.

Start with an oval curve to the base line, curving gently back up. Add a flattened curve for the top of the letter, and the main outer curve to the left of the inner oval. Splay the ends and add hairline serifs.

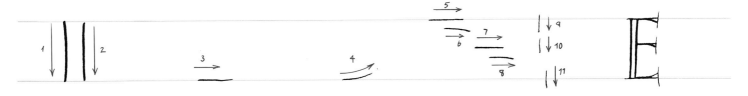

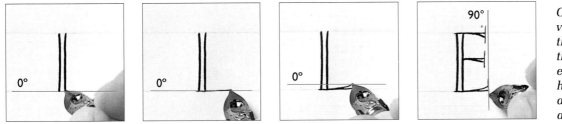

To the first two stem strokes of the "D", add a hairline curve traveling horizontally before curving to the base line. Another hairline horizontal joins it. The outer curve is then added to the bowl and the letter filled in.

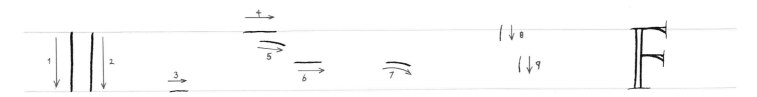

Construct two waisted vertical downstrokes and add three horizontal arms with the pen at 90°. Splay out the ends of the arms and add hairline serifs. The middle arm should be slightly above halfway.

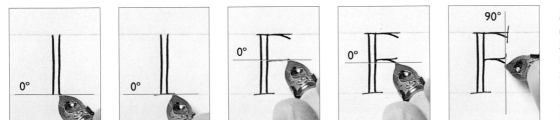

Start again with two vertical downstrokes, adding a hairline serif at the bottom. For the horizontal arms, the pen is held at 90° and pulled to the right. Gentle curves and hairline serifs complete the two arms.

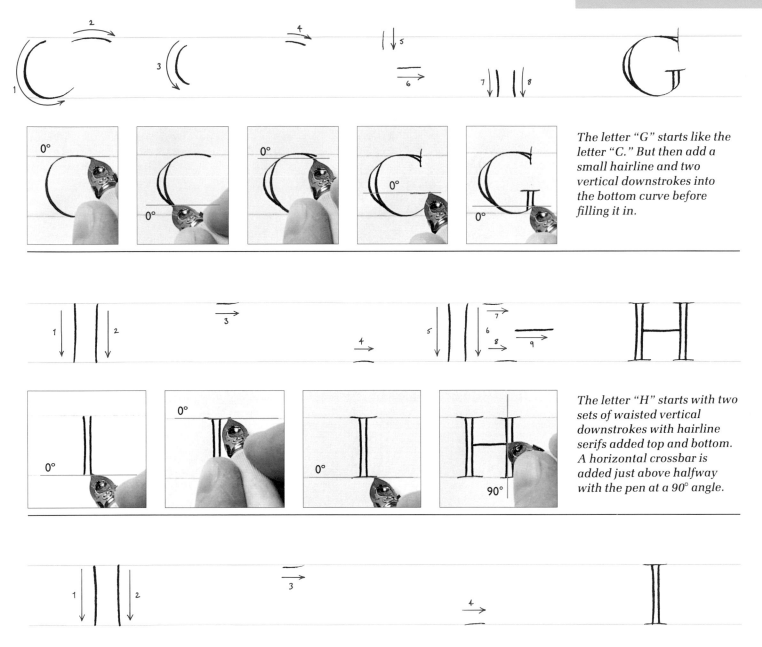

The letter "G" starts like the letter "C." But then add a small hairline and two vertical downstrokes into the bottom curve before filling it in.

The letter "H" starts with two sets of waisted vertical downstrokes with hairline serifs added top and bottom. A horizontal crossbar is added just above halfway with the pen at a 90° angle.

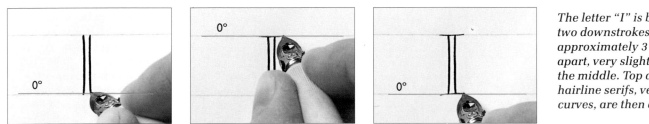

The letter "I" is built up of two downstrokes approximately 3 nib widths apart, very slightly waisted in the middle. Top and bottom hairline serifs, very fine curves, are then added.

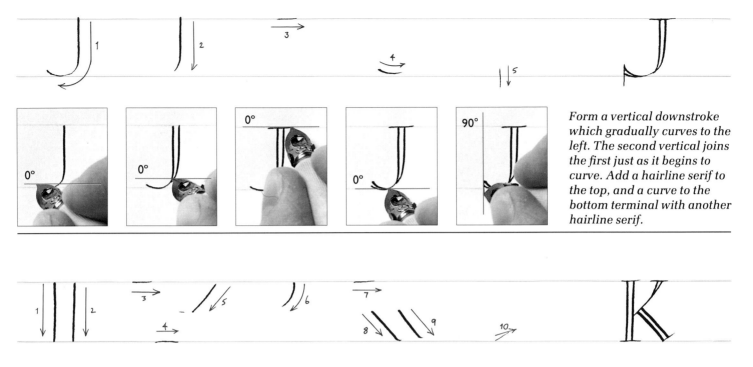

Form a vertical downstroke which gradually curves to the left. The second vertical joins the first just as it begins to curve. Add a hairline serif to the top, and a curve to the bottom terminal with another hairline serif.

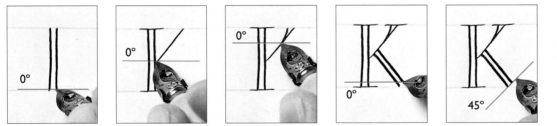

To the stem of the "I," add the inner diagonal coming into its center; splay the end and add a hairline serif. Take the lower diagonal from the first at right angles, add another diagonal and a hairline serif.

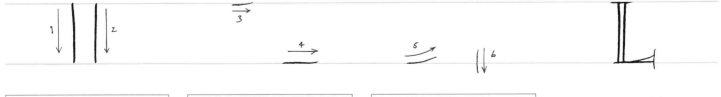

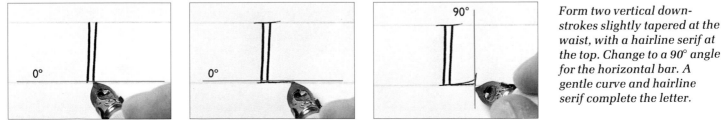

Form two vertical down-strokes slightly tapered at the waist, with a hairline serif at the top. Change to a 90° angle for the horizontal bar. A gentle curve and hairline serif complete the letter.

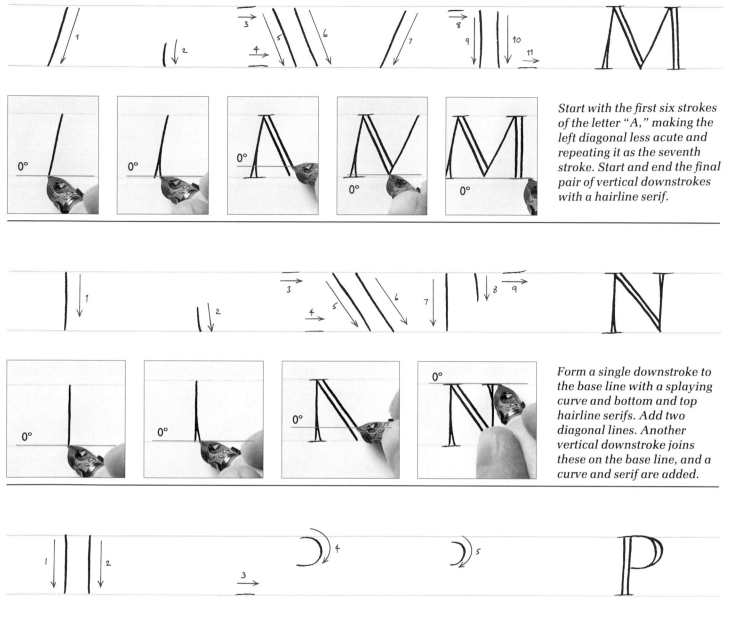

Start with the first six strokes of the letter "A," making the left diagonal less acute and repeating it as the seventh stroke. Start and end the final pair of vertical downstrokes with a hairline serif.

Form a single downstroke to the base line with a splaying curve and bottom and top hairline serifs. Add two diagonal lines. Another vertical downstroke joins these on the base line, and a curve and serif are added.

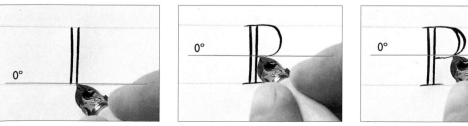

Begin with the usual vertical stem and serif. The inner counter of the bowl starts as an extended top hairline serif and progresses into a curve to rejoin the stem just below halfway. The outer curve completes the letter.

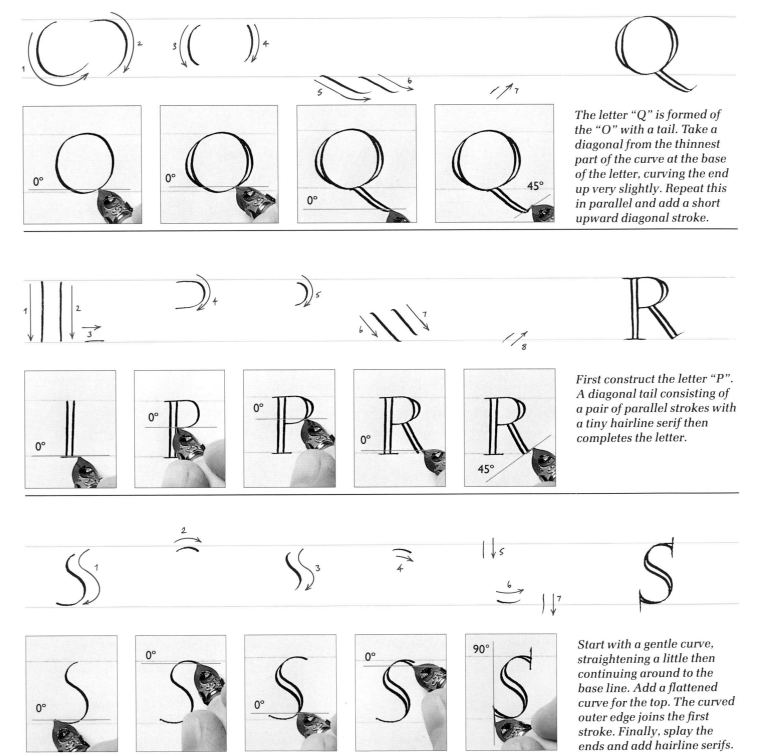

The letter "Q" is formed of the "O" with a tail. Take a diagonal from the thinnest part of the curve at the base of the letter, curving the end up very slightly. Repeat this in parallel and add a short upward diagonal stroke.

First construct the letter "P". A diagonal tail consisting of a pair of parallel strokes with a tiny hairline serif then completes the letter.

Start with a gentle curve, straightening a little then continuing around to the base line. Add a flattened curve for the top. The curved outer edge joins the first stroke. Finally, splay the ends and add hairline serifs.

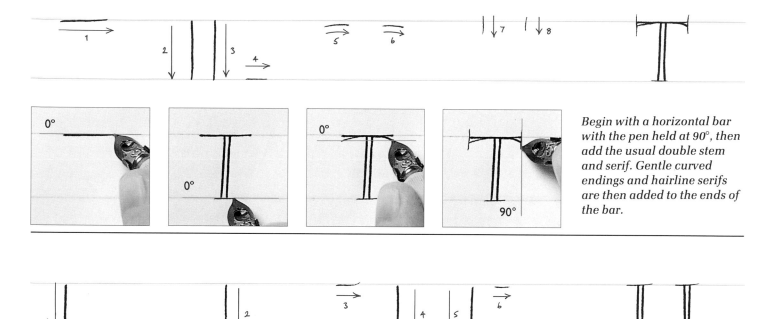

Begin with a horizontal bar with the pen held at 90°, then add the usual double stem and serif. Gentle curved endings and hairline serifs are then added to the ends of the bar.

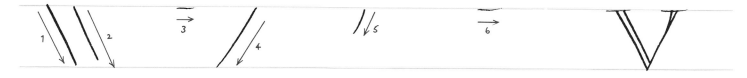

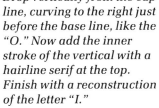

Drop vertically from the cap line, curving to the right just before the base line, like the "O." Now add the inner stroke of the vertical with a hairline serif at the top. Finish with a reconstruction of the letter "I."

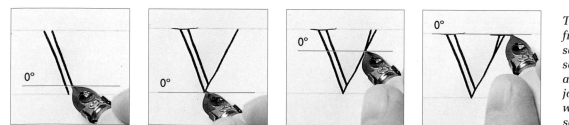

The first two diagonals run from cap line to base line; the second is shorter. A hairline serif joins them at the top, and the opposite diagonal joins them at the bottom. End with a curve and hairline serif at the top.

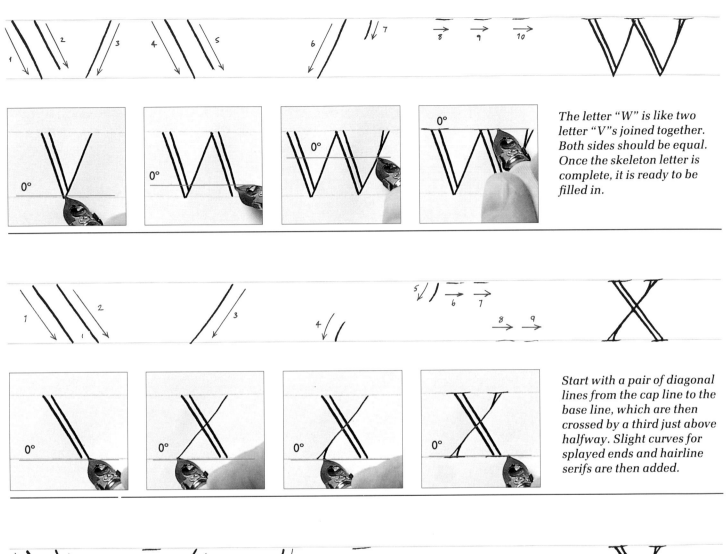

The letter "W" is like two letter "V"s joined together. Both sides should be equal. Once the skeleton letter is complete, it is ready to be filled in.

Start with a pair of diagonal lines from the cap line to the base line, which are then crossed by a third just above halfway. Slight curves for splayed ends and hairline serifs are then added.

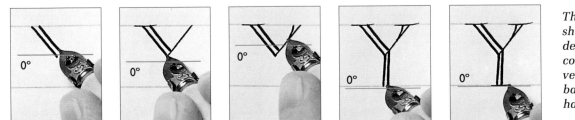

The letter "Y" starts as a "V" shape, but is only half the depth. The letter is then completed by a pair of vertical downstrokes to the base line, ending with a hairline serif.

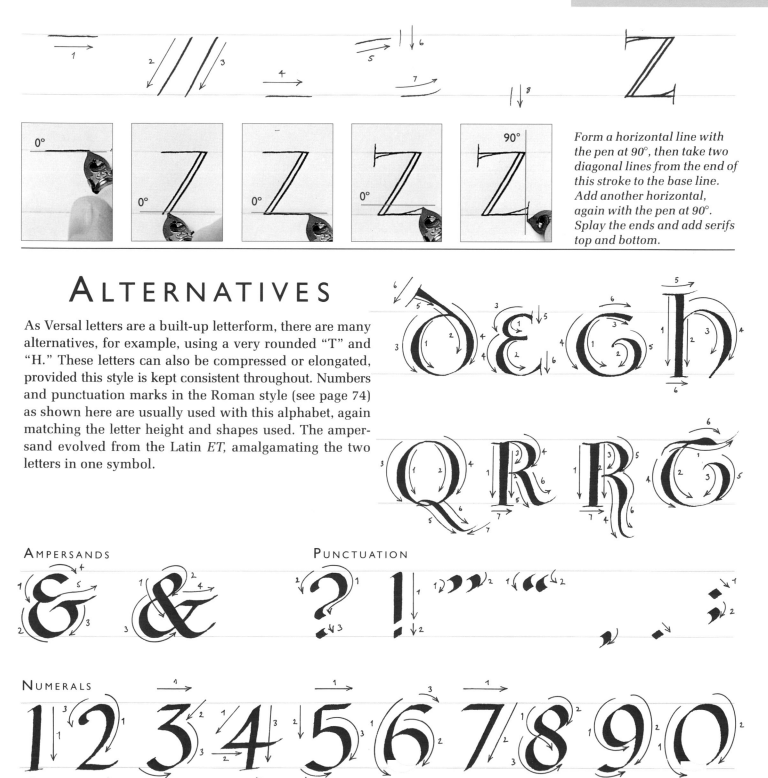

Form a horizontal line with the pen at 90°, then take two diagonal lines from the end of this stroke to the base line. Add another horizontal, again with the pen at 90°. Splay the ends and add serifs top and bottom.

ALTERNATIVES

As Versal letters are a built-up letterform, there are many alternatives, for example, using a very rounded "T" and "H." These letters can also be compressed or elongated, provided this style is kept consistent throughout. Numbers and punctuation marks in the Roman style (see page 74) as shown here are usually used with this alphabet, again matching the letter height and shapes used. The ampersand evolved from the Latin *ET*, amalgamating the two letters in one symbol.

AMPERSANDS

PUNCTUATION

NUMERALS

TROUBLESHOOTING

As the letters of the Versal alphabet are built up, there is more versatility in the size of the letters. However, it is important to keep the stems slightly wasp-waisted and not too wide and heavy, or they will lose their elegance. Make sure, too, that all serifs are hairlines, and as thin as you can make them.

The inner spaces of the letter "M" are unequal, as the first stroke was constructed too wide.

CORRECT LETTERFORMS

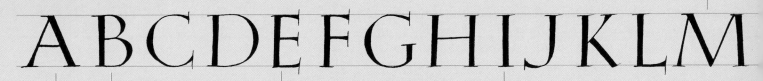

ABCDEFGHIJKLM

The top curves of the letter "B" are too small, which makes the counter space appear out of proportion with the rest of the letter.

The top horizontal arm of this letter "E" is a little long and makes the letter unbalanced.

The horizontal crossbar of the letter "E" is placed too high.

The stem of the letter "I" is too waisted, making the letter appear irregular.

The crossbar of the letter "A" has been positioned too high up and does not balance the letter.

S

The top curves of the letter "S" have been constructed too small and the bottom curves too large, making the letter slant backward.

×

The whole of this letter "N" has been constructed too narrow and would not fit in with the rest of the alphabet.

T

The stem of this letter "T" is too wide, and the two sides of the crossbar are unequal.

×

N
×

NOPQRSTUVWXYZ

The stem of the letter "P" has been formed far too wide; it should have been constructed only three nib widths wide.

P P
× ×

The curves of the letter "P" have been constructed too far down into the stem, which makes the counter space too large.

U
×

The first stem of this "U" is much too wide and does not balance the second stem.

GALLERY

The gallery examples of artwork on these two pages show how flexible Versal lettering can be. A rich variety of approaches has been explored, starting with bright, energetic, and very creative lettering in book form. Background textures can give an interesting effect, particularly in the examples shown, in which the calligraphers have used mixed media such as watercolor, gouache, acrylic, collage, and gold and palladium leaf.

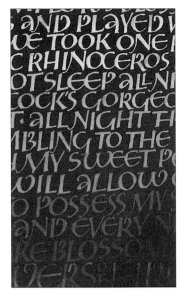

◀▼ FLOWERS OF FIRE
With experience come opportunities for presenting your work in different ways, and books are an ideal medium. Here Nancy Leavitt has chosen three poems by women. The detail (left) shows the free construction using a variety of heights, weights and bright colors to enliven the work. Pastepaper and dyed papers have been used with gouache and glair for the lettering. The work was bound using these and handmade muslin paper and presented in a cotton box lined with dyed fabric.

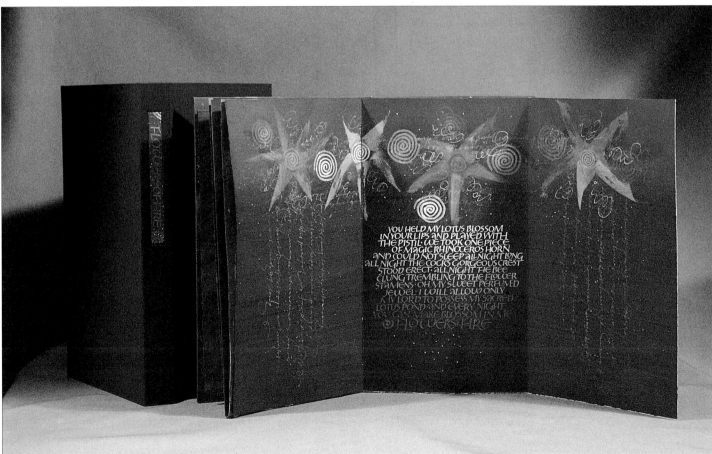

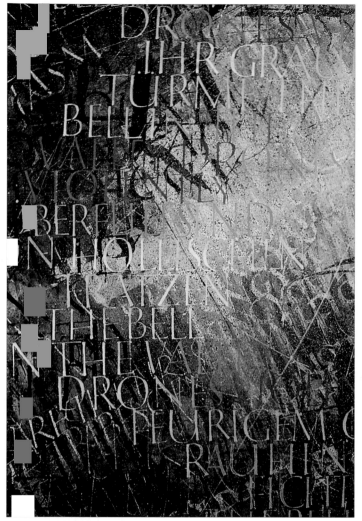

▲ THE BELL IN THE VALLEY
(DETAIL)
The background effect of Thomas Ingmire's work has been created in tones of watercolor and gouache which give a very dramatic feel to the poem by Georg Trakl called The Night. *Very finely constructed Versal letters have been used in the background and then written over each other. This highly imaginative design is a perfect interpretation.*

▼ HEBREWS II
The Bible is a wonderful source of inspiration to calligraphers, and this extract by Leana Fay from Hebrews II is no exception. Mixed media have been used to maximum effect. The whole artwork has been created on canvas using acrylics, collage and palladium leaf gilding, which gives an interesting contrast within the design. The detail clearly shows the ingenious way in which lighter lettering has been painted over much darker letters in the background, complementing the layers and creating a shadowed effect.

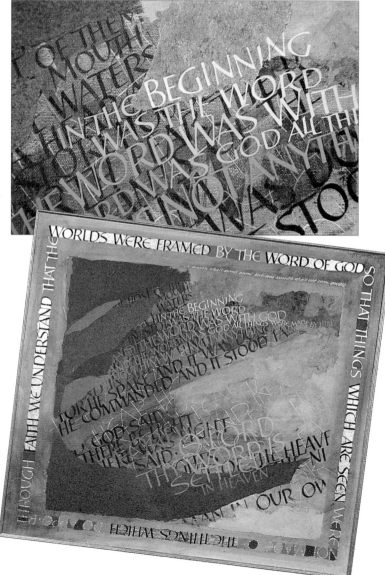

PRESENTING YOUR WORK

A good design and layout are vital to a successful piece of calligraphic artwork, so pay special attention to the ruling up and choose the paper carefully. Think about the choice of text, its tone and function, then write it in the most suitable style. Plan the layout by photocopying your lettering several times and trying out various options before deciding on the most suitable one. It is, of course, very important to keep your writing paper as clean and as neat as possible.

LETTER SPACING

The principle of letter spacing is to balance the inside, or counter shapes, of the letters with the area outside or between each letter. It is helpful to understand that, when spacing certain letter shapes, you need more space between them and, with other letter shapes, less space. Straight-sided letters optically get closer the farther away you look at them. It is the opposite with curved letters, which need to be spaced closer together.

To check whether you have spaced a whole word correctly, isolate the first three letters; the space on either side of the middle letter should appear equal. Continue by covering up the first letter, keeping the last two and adding a third, and then proceeding with the exercise, which is known as the "Rule of Three."

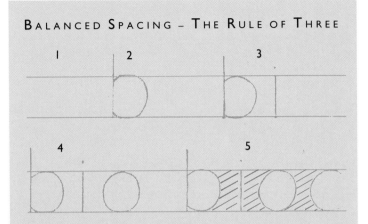

BALANCED SPACING – THE RULE OF THREE

Practicing this exercise will teach you the principles of spacing differently shaped letters.
1 Start by ruling lines ½ inch apart.
2 Draw the letter "b" as evenly as possible, as its counter area will determine the spacing of subsequent letters.
3 Add the "i" slightly closer than the width of the "b."
4 Place the "o" the same distance apart as the first two letters.
5 The letter "c" is placed slightly closer to the "o," as curved letters have more space at the top and bottom. All four letters should now look evenly spaced both inside and out.

Leave more space
between straight lines

Place curved letters closer
to straight-sided letters

calligraphy

Curved letters spaced closer

INCORRECT LETTER SPACING

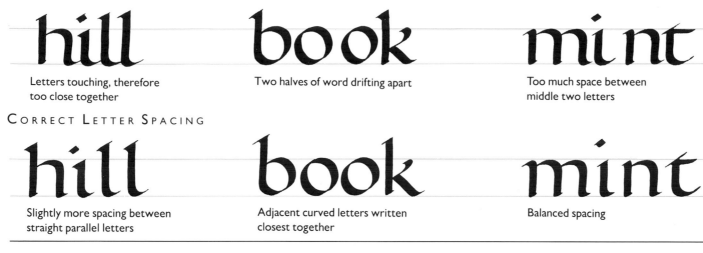

Letters touching, therefore
too close together

Two halves of word drifting apart

Too much space between
middle two letters

CORRECT LETTER SPACING

Slightly more spacing between
straight parallel letters

Adjacent curved letters written
closest together

Balanced spacing

WORD SPACING

When you have mastered letter spacing and word form-ation, you can then proceed with a sentence, this time allowing the letter "o" of the appropriate alphabet to judge the space between the words. It is a good idea to begin by practicing short sentences, because you will need to train your eye to look not only at the spacing of the letters within the word, but also at the spacing after each word. A letter "o" drawn in pencil after each word (as shown in the example below) can be very helpful to the beginner at this stage of the exercise.

In the merry month

LINE SPACING

Once you have established the writing height, enough space should be left between the writing lines so that the ascenders and descenders will not hit each other. This is known as line spacing, or interline. The usual distance for beginners is three times the x height from base line to base line, but this spacing can be reduced as you become more experienced.

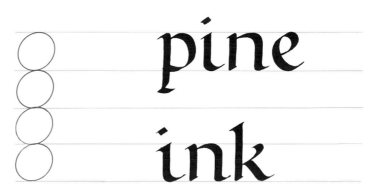

MARGINS AND LINE SPACING

Calculating margins It is usual at first to use a vertical layout, with equal margins at the top and sides and double this measure at the bottom. Then decrease the margin at the top, increase the side margins but keep them equal, and have a bottom margin double that of the top. In a horizontal layout the margins are usually widest at the sides.

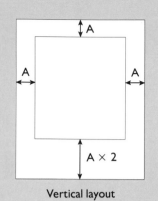

Vertical layout

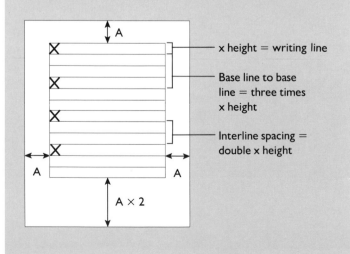

Horizontal layout

Line spacing and margins It is very important to plan your interline spacing so that ascenders and descenders do not clash. The determining factor is the writing line or x height. A distance of three times the x height from base line to base line is best to start with, giving an interline spacing of double the x height.

x height = writing line

Base line to base line = three times x height

Interline spacing = double x height

LAYOUT

Your choice of paper and layout will depend on the mood of the piece and whether it requires a formal or informal layout. Having written out the text, you should photocopy it so that you can try out various layouts. Try not to over-elaborate and remember that legibility is vital. Don't forget to allow room for the title of the work and any illustrative material. In addition to the alignments shown below, there is also justified text, where the writing aligns at the left and right edges – an effect that requires great word spacing skill to achieve. This formal approach is commonly used for prose work.

TYPES OF LAYOUT

Aligned left This layout, where all lines align vertically at the left, is very popular when line lengths are fairly even. This alignment is ideal for beginners presenting their first finished piece of work.

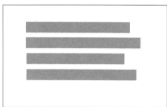

Aligned right This is a more difficult but very effective layout, especially if decoration is used on the left-hand side. Quite a lot of practice is needed to make sure that the line lengths are accurate each time.

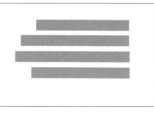

Centered This layout is ideally suited to lettering used in invitations. Draw a faint central vertical line on the page and then balance the text equally on each side of the line.

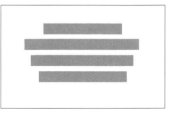

Asymmetrical Try this with more creative pieces of work, where the lines do not fit into a more conventional layout. Take care not to overexaggerate the staggered effect and thus lose the overall balanced feel.

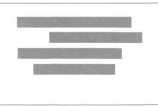

PRESENTATION

After following the advice given in the Beginners' Guide on pages 8–13 and working through the step-by-step alphabets, it is now time to put your new writing skills into practice. By now you should have a suitable degree of control for this exercise, which uses the Foundational hand, so choose a short piece of text with which to practice your presentation.

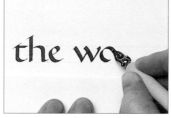

1 *Start by ruling guidelines at the usual 4½ nib widths on 11 x 16 layout paper or bond paper. Then write out your chosen text. Experiment with using larger nibs for the text heading and a smaller size for the author's name.*

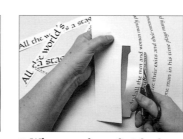

2 *When you have finished writing, photocopy the text a few times and carefully cut out the lines using scissors or a craft knife and metal ruler. Use a cutting board to protect table surfaces.*

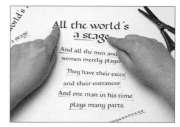

3 *Now you can move the text around to try different alignments, positions on the page, and interline spacing. Consider whether a vertical or horizontal style is best, and think about the margins.*

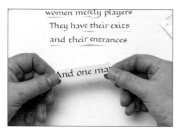

4 *Here we have decided on a centered layout. Draw the central vertical pencil line, then fold the strips of text in half and place the fold over the line to balance the text equally on both sides. Mark and rule in the guidelines.*

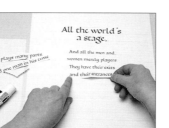

5 *Now paste the text into position line by line. Use a glue stick, or something which allows some adjustment of the paper before drying, but take care with glues which give off fumes.*

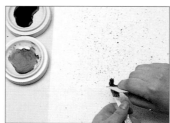

6 *To enhance your presentation, try adding a background such as paint spattering using a piece of cardboard pulled over an old toothbrush. A sponge filled with a pale gray wash can also be quite effective.*

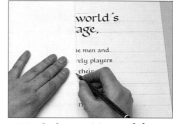

7 *Mark the positions of the ruled lines of your text along the edge of a sheet of paper.*

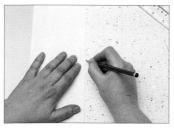

8 *Make sure the paint has dried and then transfer the marks onto your prepared writing sheet, not forgetting the central vertical line.*

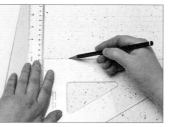

9 *Using a ruler and L-square, rule all the guidelines needed for the piece of text on the writing sheet. Take care not to smudge the paint.*

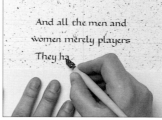

10 *Finally, copy out the text to the prepared layout, protecting your work with a guard sheet.*

11 *The finished quotation, including the author's name written smaller in capitals.*

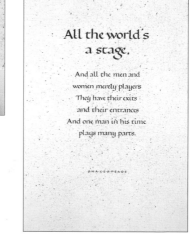

INDEX

ACKNOWLEDGEMENTS

The author and publishers would like to thank all the calligraphers
who submitted work for inclusion in the book. While every effort has
been made to acknowledge all copyright holders, Quarto would like to
apologize if any omissions have been made.

138 "Lighthouse" inspired by "Seascape" from *Elizabeth Bishop: The
Complete Poems* is reproduced by kind permission of Farrar, Straus &
Giroux, New York; *140* "Salvation" is taken from *Housekeeping* by
Marilynne Robinson, reproduced by kind permission of Farrar, Straus
& Giroux and Curtis Brown Ltd, New York; text from "The Myth of
Perfectability" taken from *Heroes in Disguise* by Linda Pastan is
reproduced by kind permission of W. W. Norton, New York and Jean
V. Naggar Literary Agency, New York; *A Natural History of the Senses*
by Diane Ackerman is published by Random House, Inc., New York;
141 "Eve: Honey in a Box" from "Eve, Long Afterwards" taken from
The Imperfect Paradise by Linda Pastan is reproduced by kind
permission of W. W. Norton, New York; *The Meadow* by James Galvin
is published by Henry Holt, New York and reproduced by kind
permission of Darhansoff & Verrill, New York; *155* "Bird of Paradise"
taken from *Collected Poems* by Robert Graves is reproduced by kind
permission of A. P. Watt Ltd, London, on behalf of the trustees of the
Robert Graves Copyright Trust, and Oxford University Press, New York.